LIGHTS, CAMERA, ACTION!

BEHIND THE SCENES, MAKING MOVIES

PHOTOGRAPHS AND TEXT BY
LOUIS GOLDMAN

INTRODUCTION BY GREGORY PECK

HARRY N. ABRAMS, INC., PUBLISHERS, NEW YORK

TO MY PARENTS AND HARRY

ON PAGE 1 *The Running Man* (1963).
Alan Bates and Lee Remick are framed in the camera's
reflex viewfinder.

ON PAGES 2 AND 3 *Tom Jones* (1963). Filming on a farm in
Dorset, England. On the horse, Albert Finney as Tom Jones;
Hugh Griffith, seated, is reading his lines off-camera.
Director Tony Richardson
is standing at the left
of the arc light.

LEFT *The Pope of Greenwich Village* (1984). The arm of
a Chapman crane at full height. DP John Bailey *(left)* and
first camera assistant Jack Brown

PROJECT DIRECTOR: ROBERT MORTON
EDITOR: TERESA EGAN
DESIGNER: JUDITH HENRY

Library of Congress Cataloging-in-Publication Data

Goldman, Louis, 1925–
Lights, camera, action!

1. Photography, Artistic. 2. Moving–pictures—
Production and direction—Pictorial works. 3. Goldman,
Louis, 1925–   . I. Title.
TR654.G635   1986   799′.9791430232   85–22835
ISBN 0–8109–1324–0

Published in 1986 by Harry N. Abrams, Incorporated,
New York. All rights reserved. No part of the contents of this
book may be reproduced without the written permission
of the publishers

Printed and bound in Japan

CONTENTS

The Chairman (1969). After a scene,
shot in Taiwan, in which he visits a school
on the mainland of China, Gregory Peck
poses with all his little co-actors.

INTRODUCTION

Looking over the masterful photographs of Louis Goldman, I am struck by the chance wisdom of a remark I made to this benevolent fanatic years ago. "Louis," said I, "your pictures are better than the movies." I spoke the truth. In single frames, Goldman captures the telling moment, the revealing gesture, stance, or attitude. It is just possible that motion-picture film, broken down into single frames, might yield pictures as packed with human interest as Goldman's. I doubt it. His art is not that of a cinematographer. His passionate energy is directed toward snaring on film, in a fraction of a second, the most intense moment of drama, emotion, humor, spirituality, pathos, ribaldry: the essence of a given scene.

Some of Louis's greatest photographs are from so-so films. They are the best of what remains from otherwise forgettable motion pictures. No matter. He wants every film to be great. There have been times, on location in remote parts of the world, when we were able to see Louis's proofs quickly—not so with the film rushes. Judging by his photographs, we invariably thought we had an epic in the making.

Goldman is a director-lover. I don't quite share his enthusiasm. I am a writer-lover. My view is that the script is ninety percent of the movie. Naturally, there are exceptions. I have worked with a few men for whom I would walk through fire: Raoul Walsh, Henry King, Bill Wellman, and Willie Wyler. I have worked for some of the "greats" who were as helpless in dealing with a flawed script as any journeyman. I have worked with famous directors who know a great deal about film technique, very little about human nature, and nothing at all about the acting craft. They are the poseurs and prima donnas of the trade, and they are well advised to work with writers and producers who can provide them with good scripts and with actors who know their business.

I offer these gratuitous opinions to add a little salt and pepper to this Introduction.

When Goldman goes to work on a movie, he has to cope with a director who may or may not understand—or who may obstruct—what he is trying to do. When I go to work, I have to cope with a script. If I get some help or inspiration from the director, God bless him, but I don't depend on it.

To return to the photographs of Louis Goldman: They are a brilliant record of a man's lifelong passion for his work. Every picture hits the bull's-eye. If only the movies had all been as good as the photographs....But then, it is a well-known fact that we can't have everything.

GREGORY PECK

19 June, 1985

BE MY GUEST

During the twenty-five years that I worked as a still photographer on nearly seventy major feature films, I was constantly struck by a paradox: The general public is fascinated by movies but knows little of what it takes to put one on the screen. This book is meant to give the reader an idea of the tremendous amount of skill, energy, ingenuity, money, dedication, toil —and at times lunacy—which go into a creative effort that awes me to this day.

The making of a big-budget, big-cast, big-screen feature requires the talents of a vast team, but I have not attempted to cover every craft or each aspect of an extremely arduous and complex process. That process may begin—a year or two before the cameras actually roll—with the spark of an idea. The story is then enlarged into a script that is subject to countless revisions. Negotiations for casting, financing, producing, and directing follow. And when the cameras have stopped, the labors involved in editing, scoring, promoting, and distributing the movie may take the better part of another year.

Once the production is approved, a huge apparatus is set in motion. It is not unusual to have, besides the cast, a crew of eighty to a hundred people working on the set: producer, director, production assistants, assistant directors, director of photography (DP), camera operator, camera assistants, carpenters, riggers, gaffers, grips, art director, set designer, set decorators, production designer, painters, prop masters, hairdressers, makeup artists, costume designers, wardrobe people, production manager, special-effects people, technical adviser, stunt men, fight coordinator, choreographer, dialogue coach, music supervisor, video consultant, documentary shooting crew, location manager, scriptwriter, continuity person, and sound technicians. In addition, there are the office staff, the accounting, transportation, editing, and publicity departments and the stars' personal aides. When scenes involving exteriors are shot, police may be needed to divert traffic and control a gawking crowd. Local officials must sometimes placate irate residents who find the presence of a film unit disruptive. Medical personnel are on hand in case of accidents, and, of course, the cast and crew must be fed.

Finally, but very much in the middle of things, is the still photographer. His very presence in this formidable machinery is incongruous. He is a misfit. Of all the assembled technicians, he is the only one who does not contribute directly to what finally appears on the screen. Even the village idiot, who may be hired to clear the set of stray bubble-gum wrappers or Styrofoam cups before a take on some remote location, contributes something. And yet, remaining on the fringe of the general pandemonium but working closely with directors, cast, and crews provides a unique vantage point, one from which I could observe the world of the movies intimately, yet realistically. Those directly involved tend to lose perspective and perceive filmmaking as the universe's top priority. If similar amounts of talent, money, and single-minded devotion were applied in all other fields, by now war, famine, and pestilence would have been wiped out.

It's a world apart: In this furnace of creation, the egos are super, the work grueling, the excitement unparalleled, the blunders colossal, the salaries fabulous, the pressures unrelenting, the waste enormous, the outbursts thunderous—and sometimes the results justify it all.

Outsiders are not often permitted to watch the shooting of a movie at close range or for long enough to get an inkling of all this. On exterior locations, visitors must watch from behind ropes at a safe distance, and on interior sets, they have to get clearance or be someone's guest.

In this book, *you* are my guest.

Willie and Phil (1980). In a small courtyard of Greenwich Village, New York, Paul Mazursky rehearses with Ray Sharkey, Margot Kidder, Michael Ontkean.

The Running Man (1963). Sir Carol Reed with Alan Bates and Lee Remick

DIRECTORS AT WORK

If the camera is Queen, then the director of a major feature is God Himself, and all the actors and highly specialized technicians around him have but one function: to do his bidding. They will do almost anything to give him exactly what he wants.

Filmmaking is above all a team effort, but the director is the one most responsible for the finished product. He must answer to the producer, of course, and to the studio that finances the picture. He must bring it in on time, within budget if possible. But responsibility for the artistic success of the movie is almost entirely his. From the moment he is selected for the job, he is completely in charge. In the preproduction stage, more likely than not, he will work with the writer on countless script changes and have the final say in the selection of locations, cast, crew, costumes, sets, props, and the myriad elements necessary to tell the story. Throughout the shooting itself, his word is the Law. But, above all, he has a definite conception of the picture, a master plan for what its "feel," tenor, and pace will be.

A cliché—perhaps as old as the industry itself—claims that movies are a director's medium. True, for in no other form of staged entertainment does the director have such total control. A play, for instance, is fine-tuned continuously until opening night, but once the curtain rises, the actors take over and have the flexibility to vary interpretation and timing at each performance. In a movie, however, you see precisely what the director wants you to see and only in the way he wants you to see it. There are rare exceptions, such as when contractual limitations or engagements elsewhere prevent the director from working on the editing of the final cut.

Consider now, if you will, what a director's job entails: total concentration; the ability to keep track of an inner vision that becomes chopped up into a thousand disconnected short pieces; the leadership necessary to mold an army of technicians into a smoothly functioning unit; the talent to extract the best performances from a large and diverse cast; the strength to face constant pressure, conflict, and crisis while remaining levelheaded; and the self-assurance to prevail against dissenting opinions from powerful studio executives. Such continuous physical and mental stress has caused many a director to collapse.

The task is herculean, but the director has awesome power to carry it out. Despite the presence of many people milling around on a set, no one has to ask who the director is. Everyone just knows. Others clear a path for him when he walks by, surrounded by a cluster of assistants who hang onto his every word, and who are trained to carry out his orders with the swiftness and efficiency of unleashed Doberman pinschers. He has the power to dismiss anyone on the spot— even actors—and start all over again if necessary. He can ask for rehearsals on Sundays, late meetings with personnel exhausted after twelve hours on the set, screenings at any time, special cameras, effects, equipment, people—anything. There is very little that he considers impossible. If, after eighteen takes, with cast and crew melting in the desert heat, he still is not satisfied, he just says, "From the start," and nobody will protest. Coffee is brought to him regularly, prepared "just so," without his ever having to ask for it; his special chair appears, as if by magic, wherever he decides to settle. And nobody else ever ever sits in that chair.

During a movie production many things can go wrong, causing irritating delays, but the greatest frustration for the director comes from the fact that in the realization of a deeply personal concept, much must be delegated to others. It takes enormous authority and experience to overcome all the pitfalls, and even then, the end result is not always what the director had hoped to achieve. Compromises are often necessary.

The ways in which directors create films are reflections of their styles and personalities. Sir Carol Reed, for instance, was the gentlest of souls. During the shooting of *The Running Man*, I never heard a loud word from him. He always spoke in a whisper, which gave additional emphasis to everything he said and created an aura of quiet respect. I once had the set for a few precious minutes between takes to photograph Alan Bates and Lee Remick. Inadvertently, Sir Carol and his assistants walked into the shot. I stepped aside to allow them to block the next scene. Suddenly, he realized I was waiting, excused himself, and moved his entire retinue out of my way. The movie was not a success, which must have been a bitter disappointment to Sir Carol after the international acclaim he received for *The Third Man*. Directors are sometimes under contract to do a specified number of films for a studio, and their hearts may not be in each one of them.

John Huston has tremendous prestige. He wears the halo of greatness, the result of having classics like *The Maltese*

Falcon, Treasure of the Sierra Madre, The Red Badge of Courage, The African Queen, Moulin Rouge, and more to his credit. Although he has since made no films that equaled those successes, he automatically establishes pride of association in his crews and elicits a vast reservoir of good will. He instills authority by his mere appearance. Towering over everyone else on the set, his craggy face a photographer's delight, always dressed in a safari jacket, and smoking black cigarillos, he can spellbind a group for hours and easily upstage any star with his fascinating stories, told in a sonorous voice. On the set of *The Bible,* it was amusing to see the producer, Dino De Laurentiis, barely five feet tall, trying to communicate with Huston in animated Neapolitan Italian, craning his neck up while Huston calmly looked down and listened. Soon they found it easier to converse when both were squatting.

Huston has the serene manner of a man who has experienced everything, and he never loses his composure. I was present when he realized that two days of complicated shooting would have to be redone because the cameraman misunderstood his request for a special filter effect. Huston brooded over the disaster by himself for a moment, shaking his head sadly. Then he puffed on his cigarillo and said, "All right, let's plan it for the beginning of the week." On a day-to-day basis he maintains a certain aloofness, and unlike other directors he does not constantly immerse himself in the script. Between takes he prefers to sit alone in a corner and do crossword puzzles.

On *Tom Jones* the crew was inspired by the sheer enthusiasm and exuberance of Tony Richardson. When the filming of a scene went well, Richardson had difficulty containing himself. He would clench his fists and pound them on his thighs, a broad smile splitting his face. Then, as soon as he yelled "Cut" he would flail his arms, like a young bird trying its wings, and shout: "Sewpah, simply sewpah!"

His excitement infected everyone. For the public-hanging scene in the film, several hundred extras were dressed up like the low-class sensation seekers, ruffians, pickpockets, and assorted misfits who used to gather at such events. While moving among them suggesting bits of action here and there, Tony got an idea that he thought would add an extra touch of authenticity. He jumped on a cart and, using a loud-hailer, asked everyone with false teeth to remove them. In a wave of laughter, bridges and dentures came out. At another time during the filming of *Tom Jones,* the whole company was caught in the woods in a torrential downpour. We took cover, and after being immobilized for an hour we heard the incredible news that we were going to shoot in that rain. During the delay, Richardson had improvised a scene in which Albert Finney was to wade through a pool of slime and pick some flowers to demonstrate his love for Susannah York. The crew and cast did not mind getting soaked to the bone, and afterward everyone walked back to the cars singing merrily.

Requiem for a Heavyweight was Ralph Nelson's first major feature, and he had to direct Anthony Quinn, Jackie Gleason, and Mickey Rooney, a trio of seasoned veterans who between them had a century of experience and some very strong ideas. Nelson was at a distinct disadvantage, and he found it difficult to assert himself. It has been suggested that when three actors of such caliber get together, the scenes practically direct themselves, but what mattered in this case is that Nelson was adroit enough to steer the right course and come in with a very good picture.

Despite his denials, Otto Preminger is indeed a tyrant on the set. His method is based on intimidation, which he has elevated to the status of a fine art. He will pick on someone who, he knows, will neither talk back nor quit. Then, at the slightest mistake, but often without even that excuse, he will summon the target at a time when the whole crew is present and subject him to a humiliating diatribe. For maximum impact, Preminger brings several personal features into play. To begin with, he wrinkles his bald pate into thick folds. Then, his face turning crimson, he moves in, stopping just two inches short of the victim's petrified eyeballs, and proceeds to hurl an avalanche of reprobation delivered in his heavy-artillery Teutonic accent—with the volume turned up to Full.

The effect is immediate and very rewarding to Preminger: Since no one wants to undergo that treatment, the crew becomes twice as efficient and the director is content. The pain he has inflicted on one individual doesn't count; only the results on the screen do. It's a masterful performance to watch, but something else again to experience. I know, having often been subjected to his outbursts. "You must understand," he told me once, "I have nothing against you. In fact I like you and respect your professionalism, but I must set an example to maintain discipline. Sloppiness is in human nature. I have to demand a hundred and twenty percent if I hope to get eighty." Subsequently, he would extend special favors to me, but a scar is a scar, however elegant the Band-Aid.

Preminger's technique is applied to anyone who incurs his displeasure. During the filming of *The Cardinal*, Preminger felt that a certain actor could perform better, and he kept whittling away at him until the poor man had to be hospitalized with a nervous breakdown. To Preminger, any deviation from what he expects is sabotage. He was shooting a difficult *Exodus* scene in Haifa: a ship, overflowing with desperate Jewish refugees, was arriving in port; the pier was bristling with British soldiers who were under orders not to let the refugees disembark. Such a large-scale setup requires the precise coordination of intricate camera movements and crowd action. Everything was finally worked out and the camera was rolling when, on the horizon left of frame, there suddenly appeared the gleaming white SS *Shalom*, loaded with tourists and heading for her home port after a fourteen-day crossing from New York. Boiling with indignation,

Preminger sent an assistant to summon the director of the port, no less. When the official arrived, Preminger erupted in a spectacular rage in front of hundreds of startled extras. He demanded an explanation. Why had the transatlantic liner not been diverted or kept out at sea? Was the man not aware that his negligence had ruined the shot? So furious was Preminger that I feared the stress combined with the fierce noonday heat would bring on a heart attack.

It is said that Preminger will back down when challenged, but I have seen it happen only once. After swallowing needling remarks for days, Lee J. Cobb finally exploded in Preminger's face, calling him, among other things, a slave driver totally devoid of common decency. In the quiet afterglow of that altercation, a cynical electrician pointed out to me that Cobb had waited for his last take on the day before his departure to blow his top.

I heard of one other half-hearted attempt by someone to speak his mind. A scene from *Bunny Lake Is Missing* was being shot in a crowded London pub, and Preminger was directing from a high platform. As the scene was in full swing, a stranger walked in from the street, looked up, declared in full range of the camera and microphones: "Preminger is a big shit," turned around, and left. General consternation. "Cut! Cut!" An assistant recovered from shock and dashed out. He reappeared and reported that the mysterious intruder had sped off in a waiting taxi. "A pity," said Preminger, seldom at a loss for words. "I would have invited him for dinner; the man has some interesting opinions."

Otto the Terrible is probably best known for his temper, but that is by no means the full measure of the man. He can be charming, urbane, witty, erudite, and he is a popular guest on radio and TV shows. He takes a personal interest in everyone on his crew. The job of directing is enough for any one man, but Preminger also produced most of his movies, totally controlling everything from the crew's lunch boxes and the stars' contracts to international press coverage. So thorough is his supervision that any mishap is unthinkable. Some donkeys that had been used in a scene in *Exodus* were being brought back to a nearby village for the night while a tender moment between Paul Newman and Eva Marie Saint was being filmed on a hilltop in Galilee. The soft twilight and the silent landscape were perfect. Suddenly, in the middle of the romantic dialogue, the braying of donkeys came rolling over the hills, completely shattering the mood. Preminger turned to his first assistant and inquired: "Jerry, are these ours?"

Preminger's capacity for work and his physical endurance are phenomenal. He can put in a full day on the set, then drive to another location to set up the next morning's shot, go back to his hotel to watch the rushes, wine and dine government officials, retire to his suite to go over a stack of bills, follow this with long-distance calls late into the night—about his upcoming movie—and go through equally grueling schedules day after day.

Critical evaluation of his skill as a director varies, but there can be only one rating as a producer: top. His pictures are completed on time and within budget, if not actually ahead and under. Even with the best planning, unpredictable and costly delays usually occur on major productions. Yet, on *Exodus*, facing three months of shooting, all on location in Israel and Cyprus where no major feature had ever been made, he had the chutzpah, on the first day of shooting, to put tickets on sale in New York for a specific date that was only seven months away—a very short time in which to film, edit, and score a movie that ran for almost four hours. It opened as scheduled. At the same time, Preminger managed to direct a Broadway play, *Critic's Choice*, which opened two days before *Exodus*. Now, that's style.

Preminger's tour de force generated attention, something he is very good at. Witness the posters he commissioned Saul Bass to create for his movies and the casting of attorney Joseph N. Welch of McCarthy hearings fame as the judge in *Anatomy of a Murder*.

Total showman that he is, Preminger never overlooks anything that can be milked for publicity. And yet, when he decided to forgo the Production Code Seal for several of his movies rather than agree to requested changes; when he officially hired scriptwriter Dalton Trumbo, who had been on the Hollywood blacklist for years, obliged to write under a pseudonym; when he battled in court to stop the TV networks from arbitrarily cutting his movies to accommodate commercials, he was motivated more by strong convictions about artistic freedom in a democratic society and a genuine abhorrence of censorship than by a desire to capitalize on controversy.

Working with Federico Fellini is a completely different experience. To begin with, there is no script, only a page or two of outline. Fellini does not organize his ideas in precisely catalogued form, establishing shots, medium shots, and close-ups. He relies on imagination and inspiration when he creates his screen images. Nor is there any definite shooting schedule. On *Fellini—Roma*, for instance, we would all meet at 8:00 A.M. in some little piazza. Fellini and Giuseppe (Beppino) Rotunno, the DP, squint at the light, survey the location. They aren't satisfied. So, everybody gets back into the cars and trucks, and the whole convoy meanders through Rome in search of another location. Fellini wonders whether it might be worth trying an exterior shot of the Admiralty. The convoy stops. Fellini likes it. Okay, everybody out. Setting up the crane and doing a little shooting takes the rest of the morning. Now, two hours for lunch. Instructions are to reconvene at an outdoor café in the Villa Borghese gardens. When I get there, the whole crew is spread out at little tables under the trees, still eating or leisurely sipping espressos. Fellini, very relaxed, enjoying the sunshine, is licking a gelato and chatting with some friends. We are to shoot a scene in the public garden with a group of male transvestites, but they are late, so everybody has another round of cappuccino or spumanti. It's all very simpatico, very Italian, very Fellini. Moviemaking is fun; there is no hysteria about conforming to a rigid schedule. Fellini would never be able to function under the contractual performance demands of an American-style production. If he can't get the shot today, he tries again some other time. If the money runs out, shooting is suspended, and the whole gang will meet again when more funds are available.

Fellini can work this way because he is a Living Legend.

The transvestites arrive. They are genuine: teased hair, makeup, high heels, rolling hips, handbags. They work together with Fellini in a casual way, totally free of self-consciousness, in plain view of the park's regular strollers. This little tableau reveals one aspect of the legend. His easy accessibility, his ingratiating nature, and his unique fame assure the eager participation of dwarfs, princes, mammoth mammas, striking beauties, average citizens, and the assorted eccentrics that his phantasmagorias require. He never demeans these people, and although they may be turned into grotesques, they know that the Maestro is not satirizing them, but rather the mores of a specific age or society.

To get the performances he wants out of his actors Fellini continues to talk to them during the actual shooting. He uses no direct sound; everything is dubbed in later. This technique is bliss for the still photographer. As the camera rolls, Fellini is incessantly coaching, pleading, encouraging, cursing, often with a loud-hailer, and pacing this way and that, gesticulating forcefully. A typical scene on an interior set in Cinecittà: A luscious woman stands, swaying seductively, in an open vintage car on a bridge at night. Half a dozen men in white togas are grouped around her; more men in raincoats are lined up behind the car, waiting their turn to jump in. Wind machines blow leaves across the set. Over the roar, Fellini is screaming: "Not like that, Rosella. Mamma mia! Wriggle your body more … good … Now glide your hands over your bosom … right … Wet your lips and look straight up … No good, cut, cut!" He strides over to the perspiring, trembling Rosella, his hands cupped in front of him, indignant and pained. "Stupida, what are you doing to me, heh? You want to give me heartburns? Such a simple thing: You are the Goddess of Lust in this town; all the senators have rolled over you, and you give me that angelic look? I need fire in the eyes, ecstasy! Don't get me mad. Let's go again."

Fellini returns to the camera with just a hint of a crafty little smile. His anger is not meant to be taken seriously. It's over before it's over, good-natured even, and always laced with humor.

While the technicians are gathering the leaves, he takes a reporter's notebook out of her hands (there is always someone around writing the nth definitive article-in-depth on Fellini), quickly draws a clever cartoon of a speeding train engine with a penis as a smokestack, signs it, and hands it back to her. She has been on the set for several weeks, and by now her notebook is virtually a collection of erotic art by Fellini and probably very valuable.

If an actor has too much trouble remembering lines, Fellini tells him to simply forget about them and instead count out loud. It is strange to watch a poor sidewalk sweeper unload his anti-Mussolini feelings to a Roman statue by saying "Uno-due-tre-quattro"—a touch of Fellini within Fellini. Yet it works.

A measure of Fellini's mythical stature is the presence of the youngsters, mostly foreigners, who gravitate to Rome when they hear he is working. They will sneak onto the supposedly restricted set and hang around for hours, unnoticed in the general confusion, not for a job but just to watch, hoping perhaps to witness a revelation of Fellini's genius.

He notices me and asks, "Louis, are you getting what you need?" I tell him I am disappointed that the big eating scene scheduled for this week has been postponed. "Ahhh, what a pity you weren't here for the bordello scene! But that pasta orgy will be good. I'll have a mountain of pasta, hundreds of Romans in Trastevere stuffing themselves with pasta until it comes out of their ears. I think we'll shoot in two weeks. Who knows! If not, we'll find something else to do. Stick around."

To the opposite again: Sidney Lumet. I know of no feature director who can match him for speed, precision, and efficiency. A dynamo of self-recharging nervous energy, trained in the demanding school of live TV drama, Lumet spends weeks in rehearsal before the cameras roll. By the time they do, the actors are steeped in their characterizations, the staging of the scenes has been worked out in great detail, and problems have been anticipated and resolved before they cause major delays later on when time and money are of the essence. When Lumet arrives on a set he has an exact plan: which shot comes first, which is last, which lenses will be used, and from which angle will each scene be photographed. During the actual shooting, he silently mouths every line, mirrors every expression, and watches his actors intensely, staying as close as possible to the lens. If he could, he would crawl into a corner of the lens shade and watch the scene from there.

With Lumet, falling behind schedule is unheard of and there is little, if any, overtime. *Twelve Angry Men* was shot in three weeks flat. *Prince of the City*, with a hundred speaking parts and sixty-five different locations, was completed in thirteen weeks.

Most directors need six or more takes before they are satisfied with a scene, but Lumet has everything so carefully planned that he usually gets what he wants in one take, sometimes two. On *Deathtrap* there was a very complex and dramatic shot of Michael Caine strangling Christopher Reeve. The camera, operated from a crane, had to come swooping across a section of the living room while technicians, just ahead of it, were yanking breakaway wooden pillars out of its path, and then come to rest inches away from Caine as he tightened a chain around Reeve's neck. It was rehearsed. It was shot. "That's it," said Lumet. "Next scene." One take. I couldn't believe it. If the focus was off only slightly or if something went wrong in the lab, the shot would be useless. It turned out fine, but this daredevil style of directing keeps the crew on the alert in an atmosphere of constant tension. On a Lumet movie, you need roller skates from day one until you take them off at the wrap party.

Paul Mazursky, like Sidney Lumet, is known primarily for "New York" films, but his style is more relaxed. Mazursky has been a stand-up comic and a writer for the Danny Kaye show and other TV comedy classics, so he has an endless repertoire of gags, jokes, amusing stories, and imitations of famous people that he delivers with great style, to the delight of the crew. It's his way of relieving the tension. He will, on occasion, yell at a crew member or an actor, but as soon as the scene is over he will apologize.

I have had the privilege of working with about three dozen directors. Some are strong-minded and will not tolerate interference from anyone; others encourage constant input from their actors. Some will bar everyone—even the stars—from watching the rushes, except for one or two absolutely essential key people. Others welcome the entire crew to these daily screenings and regard anyone's absence as a sign that he is not with the project body and soul. Some are humble, others are terminal cases of egotism.

For all of them, however, the moviemaking process consists of taking one exasperatingly small step at a time on the long and tricky road from concept to realization. In every other art form there is a logical progression; not so in the movies. Moviemaking is like telling a story, using only one word a day, totally out of sequence. Directors can only hope that in the end it will all come out right—smooth, interesting, and entertaining.

Only you can decide whether they have succeeded.

LEFT   *The Fixer* (1968). Shooting has stopped while director
John Frankenheimer and writer Dalton Trumbo rethink a line
of dialogue. The camera and dolly tracks point to the endless
horizon of the Puszta plain, in Hungary.

ABOVE   *Judgment at Nuremberg* (1962). Director Stanley
Kramer at the world premiere in Berlin

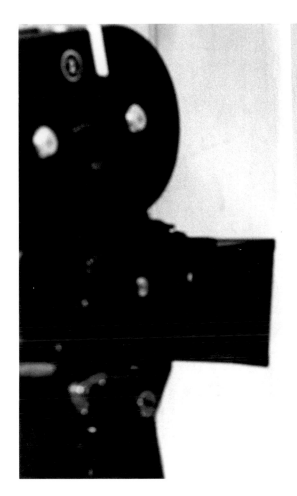

OPPOSITE *The Bible* (1965). Director John Huston has isolated himself on the set of the destroyed city of Sodom. Easily the most impressive set I have seen anywhere, it was located on Mount Etna and built entirely of lava.

ABOVE *Modesty Blaise* (1966). Director Joseph Losey in a pensive mood

ABOVE LEFT *Fellini—Roma* (1972). Fellini's hand, regulating the flow of artificial snow, seems to salute the plaster replica of an old Roman statue.

ABOVE RIGHT *Billy Jack Goes to Washington* (1976). Tom Laughlin atop a Chapman crane near the Washington Monument

OPPOSITE *The Dealing* (1972). Director Paul Williams

OPPOSITE   *The Fixer* (1968). John Frankenheimer, with Alan Bates watching, is setting up a shot in a Budapest courtyard that has been made to look like Kiev's old ghetto. The sign was made especially for the scene.

ABOVE LEFT   *The Cardinal* (1963). Otto Preminger directs a scene in the Vienna palace that was used as Nazi headquarters.

ABOVE RIGHT   *Jaws* (1975). Director Steven Spielberg explains the next shot from atop the main protagonist.

OPPOSITE   *The Alamo* (1960). John Wayne, in his first directorial effort, seems relaxed here on a night shoot—with the help of a little background music from a concertina.

ABOVE   *Moscow on the Hudson* (1984). Paul Mazursky sets up a shot in a graffiti-besmudged New York City subway car.

OPPOSITE   *The Verdict* (1982). Director Sidney Lumet and Paul Newman work out a problem in an unused corner of the courtroom set.

ABOVE   *All The President's Men* (1976). Director Alan J. Pakula is pensive before calling in cast and crew for a Washington, D.C., courtroom scene.

LEFT *The Honey Pot* (1966). Director Joseph L. Mankiewicz and a giant sunset backdrop on a stage in Cinecittà, Rome

ABOVE *The Castle* (1968). German director Rudolph Noelte

The Last Dragon (1985). It took over $500,000 and four months' work by a twenty-man construction crew to build this elaborate disco set in a Manhattan studio. It had three huge video screens and a triple centerpiece of blinking colored lights. As the centerpiece descended from the ceiling, a platform was lowered from it, revealing Vanity, the female lead. The floor, constructed of glass on a raised stage and lit from underneath by neon tubing, was built so solidly that, without shaking, it could support a crane, plus five Panavision cameras and their crews, plus, at times, a hundred wildly gesticulating dancers. The production designer was Peter Larkin. After three weeks of shooting, the chain saws reduced the set to a heap of toothpicks.

THE TECHNICAL SIDE

Comparisons between the structure of an army and that of a movie production come readily: There are the top brass (director, producer), answerable to political bodies (studios), a headquarters (production office), a hierarchy of subordinates, a battle plan, troops of skilled specialists led by battalion commanders (department heads), precisely defined areas of competence, and a strict code of discipline. Serious mistakes will not result in a court-martial—most likely, just instant dismissal.

Like the army brass, moviemakers have clout that is truly amazing. Spain, Ireland, and Yugoslavia—along with many other countries—have put their regiments at the disposal of foreign producers. When a unit arrives to shoot on location, it literally takes over. In small towns, that is not too difficult, but I have seen rush-hour traffic diverted from the centers of Paris, Vienna, Rome, Dublin, Amsterdam, Philadelphia, and New York, always with the eager cooperation of local police. And when a scene is about to be shot, even first-time production assistants just out of film school are vested with the power to prevent people from reaching stores, their cars, their apartment buildings, or even from looking out of their own windows. Pedestrians who rush about on important errands suddenly don't mind standing behind a rope for an hour just to watch a scene in which some unknown actress hails a taxi. There was fierce competition in Washington, D.C., for the discarded peel-aways from my Polaroid shots because they still had a trace of Robert Redford on them. What is the explanation for the strange behavior that movies can induce? It must have something to do with the wonderment that magic evokes, because when the lights go on again there is absolutely nothing left on that screen. And yet, just minutes before, the audience was experiencing creeping goose pimples, or shaking with laughter. Perhaps watching the making of a movie allows us to partake in a magical process.

Another similarity between the military and the movie industry is that a bewildering variety of equipment, tons and tons of it, is used by both. There are cranes that can lift a Panavision camera and three people from gutter level to a third-floor window in one swift move—or glide and swing in every conceivable direction. Entire convoys of trucks and campers are crammed with the special needs of the construction, wardrobe, camera, props, hairdressing, makeup, sound, special effects, grips, and electrical crews. The generators are capable of providing as much as 30,000 watts of illumination.

Onlookers always wonder why, even with brilliant sunshine, big arc or quartz lights of ten kilowatts each are still necessary. Strong sunlight creates strong shadows. The eye can compensate for the extreme contrast, but film cannot, so artificial light is needed to open up the shadows. Nowadays, smaller cameras and faster film that requires less light allow shooting in locations as tiny as the closet kitchens of modern Manhattan apartments. Needless to say, it can get very crowded in there. But even custom-made studio sets are always overcrowded with people and equipment.

A studio set can be an entire floor of the Washington *Post* offices (*All the President's Men*), a dingy basement (*Klute*), a bedroom inside a windmill (*Deathtrap*), or a fantasy location (*The Wiz* and the Star Wars movies): in short, any set that has to be built because it does not exist or because it is more practical to duplicate than to rent the original. Didn't New York Chinatown's famed Mott Street and adjoining sections of Little Italy look terrific in *The Year of the Dragon*? Yes, but actually they were full-scale reconstructions, created in minute detail on a back lot of the Dino De Laurentiis studios in North Carolina. Sets are erected in movable sections to allow the cameraman flexibility. From the outside, one just sees plywood held together by double-headed nails and C clamps. Inside, however, when the aim is realism, the artists responsible for set design, construction, and decor create astonishing simulations. You know you are on a set, but there is no doubt that this is the nerve center of a major newspaper or the residence of a famous playwright. When technicians arrived on the Sistine Chapel set of *The Agony and the Ecstasy*, they instinctively lowered their voices. But a set costing as much as a half-million dollars and taking months to build may be used for three weeks' shooting and then broken up by sledgehammers and discarded.

After having rehearsed the scene and discussed the various angles with his DP, the director walks away and the technicians take over. The DP's function is to interpret the director's concept in visual terms, and he alone is responsible for the quality of the image on the screen. His requirements get top priority. Directors don't like to waste an hour or more waiting until the set is ready. The scene already exists in the director's mind, but it does take time to light and dress a set just as he wants it. Frequently, directors use the time to read through the scene again with the actors.

All over the studio now there is an explosion of feverish activity. Construction grips roll away an entire wall section on wheeled platforms, shouting: "Watch your backs!" Miles of electrical and sound cables snake over, under, around, and across everything. From high up on narrow catwalks and from all around the set gaffers aim lights according to instructions from the chief electrician. During the tedious lighting process, stand-ins for the actors patiently go through their motions over and over again. Grips lay tracks for a traveling shot, making sure they are level. The boom man tries to get through with a three-wheeled Fisher boom that has a microphone dangling at the end of a long pole. Just off the set the sound mixer, sitting by his Nagra recorders and console of blinking lights, tests the clarity of the sound through his earphones. When it is impractical to record the scene with a moving microphone, sound technicians plant tiny wireless microphones right in the area being shot: behind a book or a coffee cup, under an actor's tie, or in a bra.

While the DP is lighting the set, brightening it here, shading it there, the camera assistants check the exact positions of the actors for each moment in the scene and determine their distance from the camera. The distances are marked on little pieces of tape, which are placed on the floor to enable precise focusing during shooting. The camera operator, his eye glued to the viewfinder, rehearses the panning and tilting moves required by the action and scrutinizes every square inch of the frame. The camera itself is accorded more Tender Loving Care than any star. You will never see a camera standing alone; there is always a protective ring of attendants around it. It must not get too hot; it must not get too cold; no stray light must ever hit its eye; no speck of dust must ever settle on it. Every evening it is dismantled, cleaned, oiled, and tucked away for the night on a bed of foam padding inside a steamer-size metal trunk.

The bumps in the track have now been eliminated, and the dolly grips are practicing their intricate choreography. At a specific point in the dialogue, the grips push the dolly across the room, gently raising the arm supporting camera and operator. The dolly picks up speed, then slows down, and finally comes to rest on another specific word and at a precise mark a foot away from a table. All this is executed with grace and smoothness worthy of a ballet.

In the midst of this beehive it is startling to see some people doing absolutely nothing, chatting by the coffee and doughnuts table or relaxing comfortably in a chair, busy with a crossword puzzle. It is in the nature of the business that many technicians are not needed all the time, but they are paid to be available. An idle worker could be the set painter standing by with fast-drying paint to retouch damaged areas of a wall at a moment's notice, a propman needed to light a controlled fire in the fireplace, or the editor waiting to discuss the need for additional footage for a scene that has already been shot. And if you happen to spot an incredibly stunning knock-'em-dead creature standing alone, resist the temptation to start flirting with her. Instead, take another doughnut and walk away if you want to live to work another day. Very likely she is one of the big shot's girlfriend-of-the-month, and thus untouchable.

While a hectic pace pervades the set, other departments are no less busy elsewhere. Architectural plans are being drawn to exact specifications. From them, the construction crew will erect, on another stage, a new set that will be needed in a few weeks; painters make new signs to be hung over the existing ones on an exterior location; the special-effects crew is testing the camera-worthiness of rubber scissors to be used in a stabbing attack.

In Wardrobe, the clothes for the scene being readied on the set are being taken off the racks. Months of preparation preceded this step. From sketches submitted by the costume designer for the director's approval, a final selection of wardrobe was made for every key player. Whether it be a Roman toga, a fancy eighteenth-century crinolined gown, or a pair of dungarees with holes in the knees, each was carefully chosen to "fit" the character. Clothes for the stars are custom-made, usually in duplicate to be safe. Every garment is then tagged with the appropriate scene number and the actor's name and role. Polaroid shots record the exact way the clothes looked at the end of each print. For contemporary scenes, extras are expected to bring their own clothes plus a change, so the producer gets two different background crowds out of the same people.

Such meticulous and thorough preparation is also the norm in Hair and Makeup. These two departments usually work in tandem and put the finishing touches on the actors before they step in front of the camera. But long before that moment, various hair and makeup styles were first screen-tested, and one was finally approved. Some roles require very little work, and an actress may even choose to do it herself. Others take hours, especially when aging or alterations in physiognomy are called for. For example, George C. Scott wore a full beard as Abraham in *The Bible*, and each morning it had to be painstakingly built up with separate tufts and strands; throughout the shooting day it was constantly repaired. For each one of his *Requiem for a Heavyweight* scenes, Anthony Quinn's face was modified to that of a battered boxer. More complex metamorphoses, such as those in *Planet of the Apes* or *Star Wars*, are the domain of Special Effects.

If the director wants to shoot at 9:00 A.M., actors requiring lengthy preparation have to be up before sunrise—hardly the glamorous treatment. The hair and makeup people see the stars "naked," so to speak, in a way the rest of us never do. They know their "secrets"—how to hide the flaws and enhance the good traits. They deliver the stars to the camera as the demigods that we admire. They are the ones who have skin contact, and the relationship is thus a special one. Hair and makeup people are usually privy to the stars' moods and feelings about their roles, the director, the co-stars, and the movie in general. Incidentally, the official nomenclature for the powder-puff people is Makeup "Artists" and, except for the "Scenics," they are the only technicians so designated. Their craft is more clearly defined in other languages. In French, *maquillage* (concealment, alteration designed to mislead). In Italian, *trucco* (trickery, a cheat). In German, *Maske* (a disguise, a camouflage). In any language, however, they know not only how to embellish but also how to make beautiful "ugly" faces. And even from as close as ten inches you would swear that the "wound" on an actor's leg is actually oozing pus.

To compensate somewhat for the cruel 6:00 A.M. calls, the hair and makeup room is always very cozy: bright lights, good coffee, comfortable chairs, cool in the summer, warm in the winter. No matter how primitive the location, the hair and makeup camper is the best place to be—if you are allowed in.

On the set, hammering and sawing are still going on. The art director decides that a vase doesn't look right and sends for another one. The second assistant director relays over his portable radio that the star, now in makeup, will need another fifteen minutes. The noise is such, however, that the first assistant director can hardly hear, and he shouts: "Guys, keep it down to a roar!" That plea will be effective for only a few minutes.

It seems unlikely that a motion picture ever emerges from this chaotic three-ring circus inside a pressure cooker. An electrician brought his three-year-old daughter to the set one day, and she put it best. She took it all in, bewildered and confused, craning her neck this way and that, and then the sweet little voice asked: "But Daddy, where is the movie?"

Eventually, however, everything will fall into place. There is method to this madness after all.

ABOVE *Prince of the City* (1981). The camera moves along the table on a specially built sled, its speed regulated by Sidney Lumet's arm. Chairless actors will fall away as the camera approaches.

OPPOSITE *Blow Out* (1981). Philadelphia's Independence Hall is the background for this large-scale scene of a Mummers' Day parade. The floating Liberty Bell of helium-inflated rubber was custom-made for the scene.

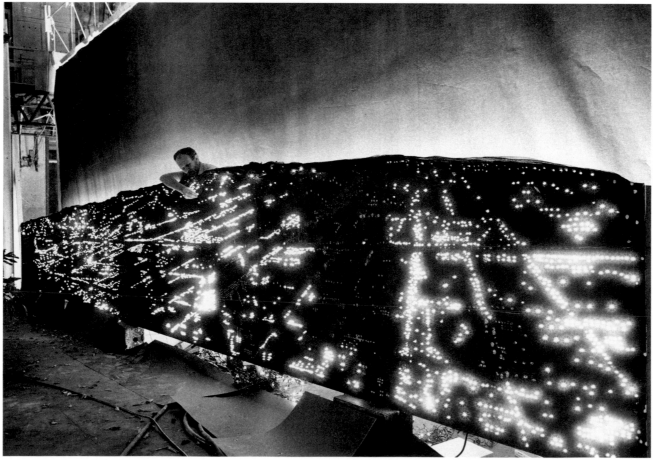

LEFT, ABOVE *Just Tell Me What You Want* (1980). Ali MacGraw and Peter Weller visit the home of a Hollywood mogul, played by Tony Roberts, on a stage at New York's Astoria Studios.

LEFT, BELOW An electrician replaces dead bulbs of "Hollywood" background.

ABOVE *The Year of the Dragon* (1985). A night scene in Chinatown's Mott Street, New York. Actually, it's a full-scale replica built on a back lot at the Dino De Laurentiis studios in North Carolina. The production designer was Wolf Kroeger. Every detail was accurately duplicated: the neon signs, the colors of the storefronts and buildings, the cracks in the pavement, and the steam emanating from manhole covers.

Fellini—Roma (1972). Fellini directs a scene in a narrow street of Rome's Trastevere quarter.

Willie and Phil (1980). Sven Nyquist, famed cameraman of Ingmar Bergman movies, sets up a shot above New York's Washington Square.

ABOVE   *Blow Out* (1981). Director Brian De Palma and DP Vilmos Zsigmond discuss a shot while the camera and crane, reflected in a glass pane, are put in position.

OPPOSITE   *Inspector Clouseau* (1968). The crew shooting in Zurich's main railroad station. The camera, mounted on a special plywood platform, is focusing on Alan Arkin.

OPPOSITE   *One-Trick Pony* (1980). Director Robert Young on location in a Manhattan high school

ABOVE   *Ulysses* (1967). On a Dublin street, Milo O'Shea as Bloom *(left)* and Maurice Roeves as Stephen Dedalus are standing by for a take, waiting for signal from director Joseph Strick.

The Bible (1965). John Huston sets up a scene for Genesis. The powerful gesture
suggests "Let there be light."

Jaws (1975). All this light artillery was needed in broad daylight to counterbalance
the deep shadows on a billboard.

OPPOSITE *Blow Out* (1981). Sixty feet above the trees and bridge below, in a special open crate, an electrician and the lights are suspended from the extended arm of a crane. Because the company was pressed for time, dinner was canceled that night, and the electrician had to remain in the crate for an uninterrupted eight hours until wrap came at daybreak.

ABOVE *Prince of the City* (1981). Cherry pickers lift strong arc lights, used to simulate sunlight for a scene in a Bronx apartment.

LEFT *Jaws* (1975). The fierce
Nor'easter wind on a Martha's Vineyard
beach forces an electrician to take cover.

OPPOSITE *Modesty Blaise* (1966).
Operator and camera: an "optical" illusion

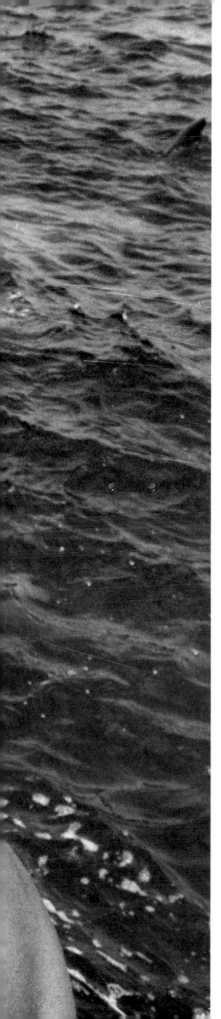

LEFT *Jaws* (1975). The mechanical shark, operated by remote control with very complex machinery, refused to work properly for a long time. When it finally did, producer Richard Zanuck showed his feelings.

ABOVE *Alfred the Great* (1969). Repellent lotions and sprays proved useless when the crew worked in a mosquito-infested swamp. DP Alex Thomson resorted to a silk stocking.

Jaws (1975). Director Steven Spielberg sets up a close look into the monster's jaws. Standing behind him are operator Mike Chapman and assistant Jimmy Cotner, both now DPs in their own right.

Hannibal Brooks (1968). A helping hand protects director Michael Winner from the elephant's swinging tail.

ABOVE *Alfred the Great* (1969). David Hemmings, holding a microphone, is handed a cigarette by a crew member. On this take, the camera will shoot another actor at the edge of the pool. The following shot will be of Hemmings as King Alfred in the pool.

OPPOSITE *Just Tell Me What You Want* (1980). Sound man Jim Sabbat and his equipment are crammed into the trunk to record the dialogue of the scene that will be shot in the moving limousine.

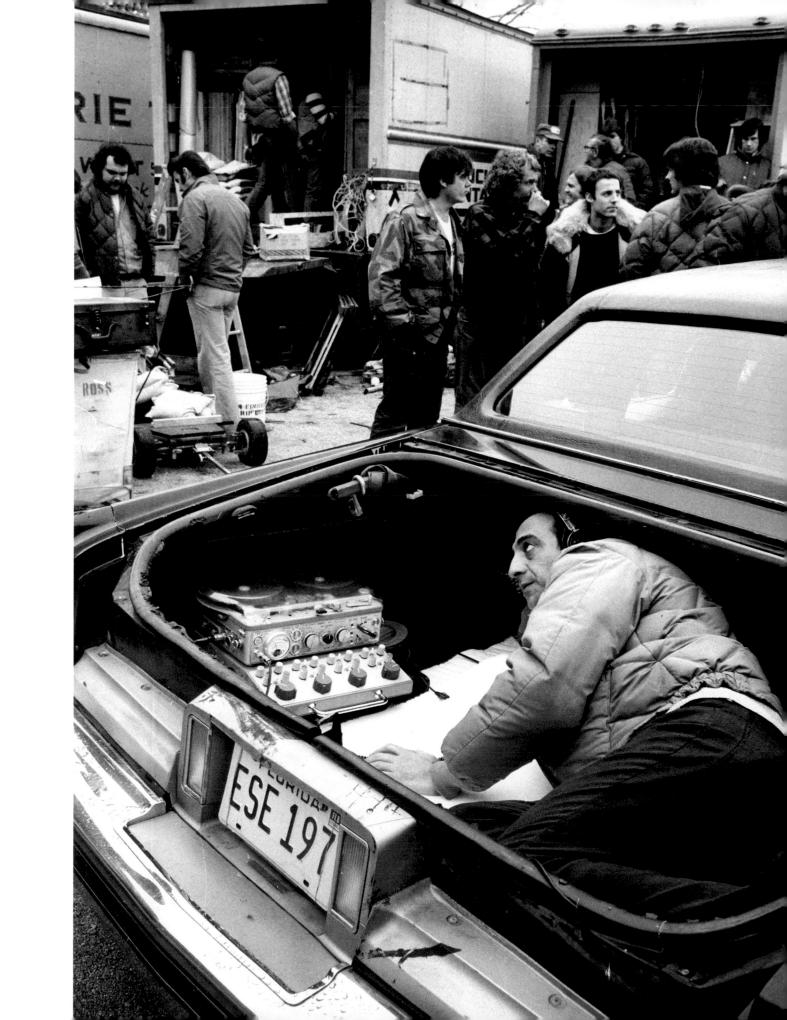

Blow Out (1981). Various methods were tried to show smoke in the beam of a home projector, until special-effects man Cal Acord found that smoking three cigarettes at once worked best.

The Wanderers (1979). A Wanderer-turned-Baldie is cornered by his former friends under an El.
Artificial smoke creates an eerie effect.

The Wanderers (1979). An elaborate installation of pipes and hoses creates artificial rain. The apparatus was so effective that the camera lens remained fogged for hours afterward.

Moscow on the Hudson (1984). Special gear protects the camera during a scene in artificial rain on a Manhattan street. Robin Williams and Maria Conchita (with newspaper) wait for "Action" from Paul Mazursky, who is standing under EXPOSED.

ABOVE *Jennifer on My Mind* (1971). Tippy Walker, hallucinating on drugs, wants to jump off the balcony rail. Boy friend Michael Brandon is trying to talk her down. A special rigging crew holds her securely with wires that are out of camera range.

RIGHT *Inspector Clouseau* (1968). Technicians have prepared Alan Arkin for a scene in which he is thrown off a speeding train in Switzerland and gets hooked like a bag of mail.

Blow Out (1981). Everybody wants to be an extra in a movie, but few realize it means long hours and boring work. These two, among the thousand needed for a night scene, are catching precious moments of sleep before being called out again in freezing weather.

Alfred the Great (1969). Dummies simulating fallen soldiers are picked up at dawn, after a night of shooting fierce battle scenes between English troops and the invading Danes.

LEFT *Requiem for a Heavyweight*
(1962). Anthony Quinn *(right)*
with trainer Johnny Ingersano in
Central Park, New York, preparing
for his role as an aging boxer.

OPPOSITE *An Unmarried Woman* (1977).
Alan Bates *(right)*, who plays a painter,
gets technical advice from painter
Paul Jenkins in his New York studio.

ABOVE *Exodus* (1960). All faces are tense as Otto Preminger rehearses with Jill Haworth and Sal Mineo in Haifa, Israel.

OPPOSITE *A Walk with Love and Death* (1969). John Huston, who directed his father, Walter, in *Treasure of the Sierra Madre*, directs his daughter, Anjelica, in this one. He also played the part of her uncle in the movie.

OPPOSITE   *A Walk with Love and Death* (1969). Director John Huston also played the part of a lord of a sixteenth-century castle. Here, in period undergarment, he is waiting for the wardrobe ladies to arrange his robe.

ABOVE   *The Hill* (1965). Director Sidney Lumet adds a touch of "perspiration" to the uniform of Michael Redgrave, who played the role of the medical officer.

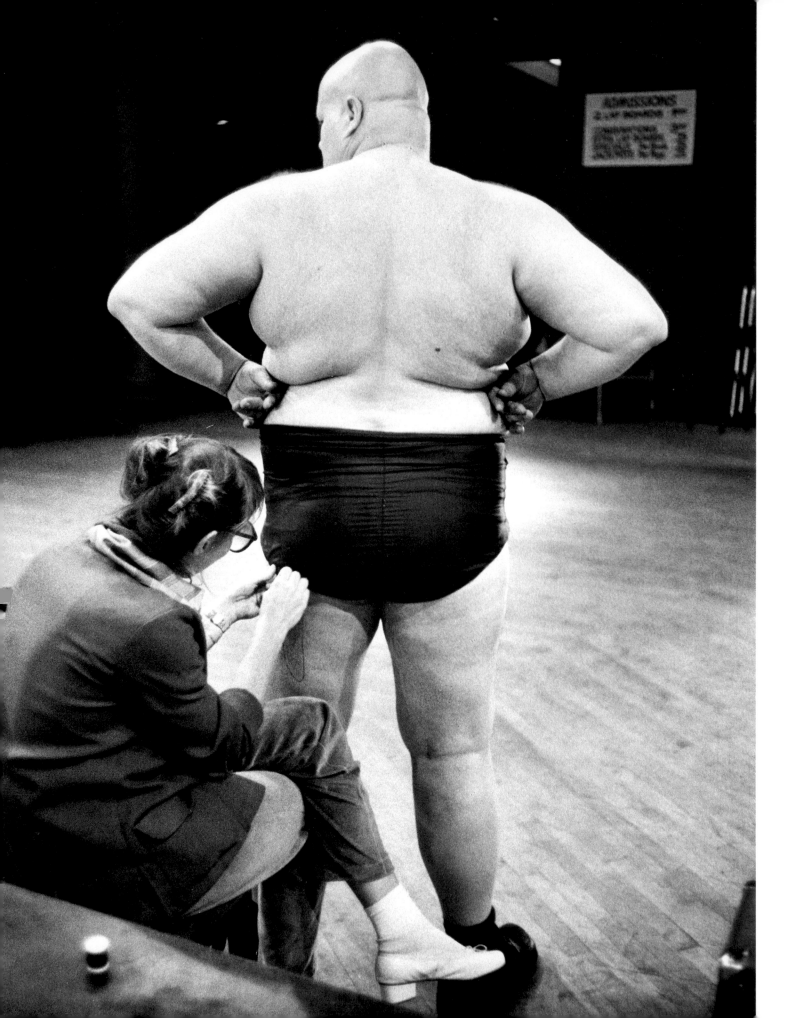

LEFT   Wardrobe lady Ellen Mirojnick
fixes wrestler Captain Haggerty's
trunks, ripped during a take for a 1978
television beer commercial.

OPPOSITE   *The Chairman* (1969). A
young actress gets body makeup for a
nude pose with her partner. They are
living statues in the House of Elegant
Pleasures, a Hong Kong restaurant built
on a Shepperton Studios stage in
England. Because of quick camera
panning, they will hardly be seen,
if at all.

Tom Jones (1963). Makeup for Albert Finney on a farm in Dorset, England

Fellini—Roma (1972). Fellini lends a hand at touching up a plaster copy of a Roman statue.

ABOVE *Fellini—Roma* (1972). Fellini, with a real-life transvestite, is getting ready for a scene in Rome's Villa Borghese gardens.

OPPOSITE *The Wanderers* (1979). Each of the "baldies" was paid $500 to shave his head and keep it that way for the duration of the shooting.

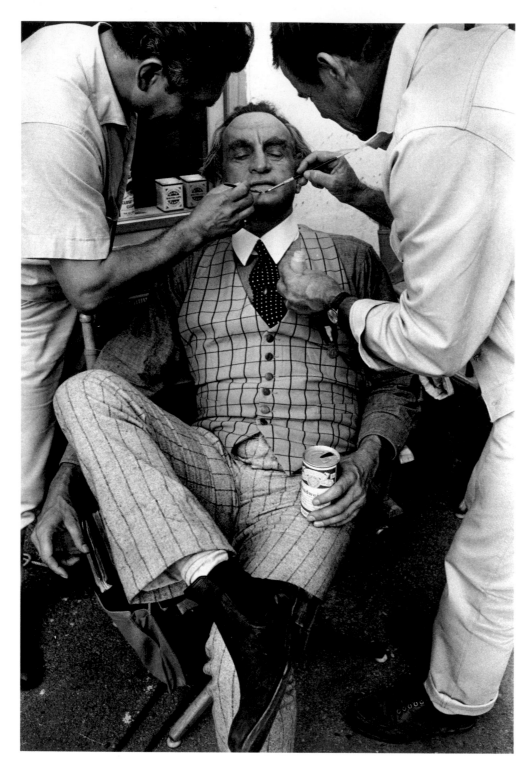

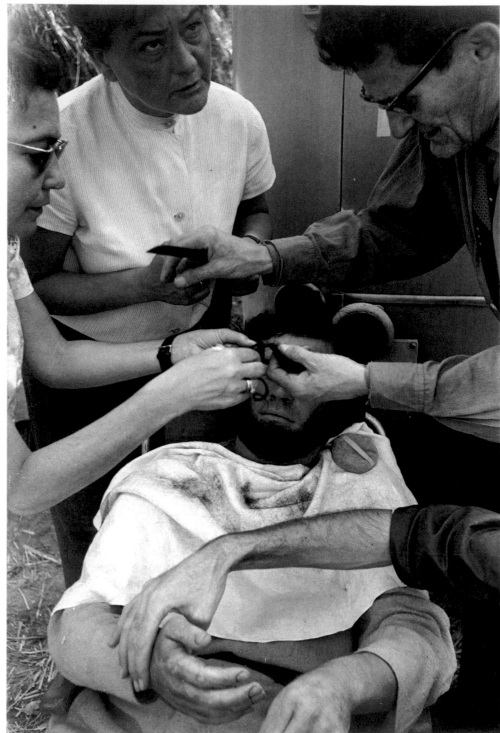

ABOVE LEFT   *The Flim-Flam Man* (1967). Layers of latex give George C. Scott's skin an older look.

ABOVE RIGHT   *The Fixer* (1968). Busy hands apply Alan Bates's fake beard each day.

OPPOSITE   *Requiem for a Heavyweight* (1962). To give Anthony Quinn the look of an over-the-hill, aging boxer, makeup artist Dick Smith, seen here applying blood before a fight scene, has almost entirely reshaped Quinn's face.

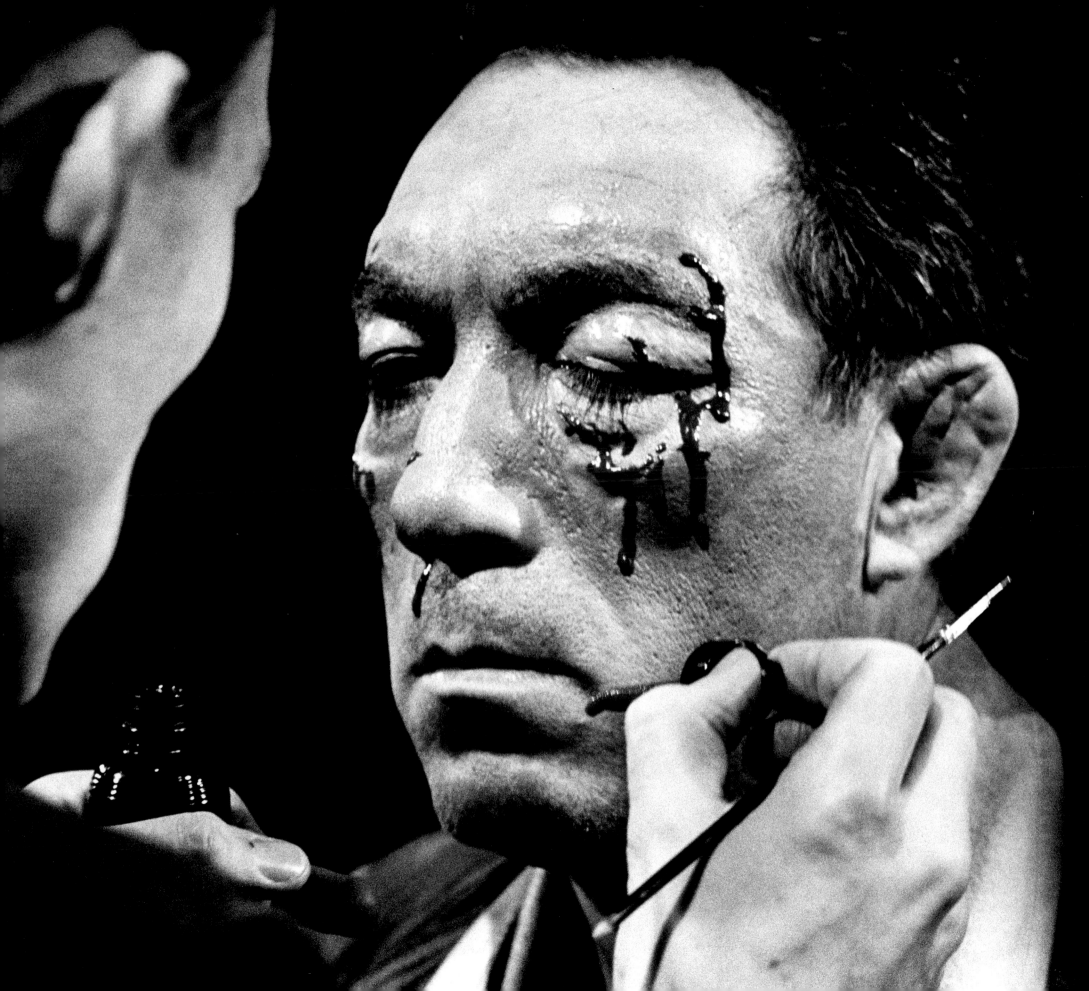

Tom Jones (1963). Susannah York wanted to hold the slate for the shot of Dame Edith Evans in an eighteenth-century carriage.

ROLL 'EM...

The technicians are finished. The area where the scene will be played is now surrounded by a nearly impenetrable maze of people and cables, metal stands, big lights, small lights, diffusion screens, white show cards, opaque black flags of various sizes to shade specific areas, double nets, single nets, and lavenders to fine-tune the intensity of the light. The set is ready.

The director asks for a full rehearsal, this time with camera. The first assistant director calls: "First team." The actors may still have tissue paper tucked in their shirt collars to protect them from makeup smudge, and the actresses wear hairpins that will come out at the last minute. The first assistant director yells: "Quiet on the set. Rehearsal." Assistant directors do a lot of yelling. Final details of performance and coordination between actors and camera are worked out. The director says, "Let's shoot it." The first assistant yells: "Shooting this time. Give me three bells." The sound man's button lets out three loud rings, the doors are shut, and the outside panel starts flashing *Silence*.

Now things get really tense. The first assistant orders: "Roll camera," the second camera assistant raises a slate showing the title of the movie, the names of the director and the DP, the numbers of the scene and take, and the date. The camera operator throws the switch, the film is running, but the second camera assistant waits for the sound mixer to shout "Speed" (meaning his tape has reached the required seven and a half inches per second) before calling out, for example, "Scene Thirty-seven, Take One," and smartly slapping down the hinged part of the slate. These visual and aural ID marks are for the editor. They indicate the exact point at which image and sound are in perfect synchronization.

And now the director gives the classic movie command: "Action!" From this moment on nobody moves except those involved in the scene. Movement distracts. And there is absolute silence. Do not sit down or get up from a chair, or even shift your weight from one foot to another on a wooden floor. The resulting squeaks could ruin the sound track or the actors' and director's concentration. Any sound may cause the director to halt the shooting, and if you're not thrown off the set, at the very least you get stares that cause permanent frostbite.

The camera keeps rolling until the director says "Cut." If he likes the take, he will say "Print," and the script supervisor and the sound recordist circle the number of that take on their reports. The entire roll of film will be developed, but only the circled takes will be printed for screening at the next day's rushes.

Right after "Cut," the first assistant shouts, "Back to starting position," whether we are going again or not, and everybody rushes in to set things up again for the beginning of the scene. All may go well on the first take. Or the director may still not be satisfied by the tenth. Why would a well-rehearsed scene need ten or more takes? Watch.

The scene, let us say, is in front of a housing project on a sunny day. Eddie, a young off-duty policeman in civilian clothes, is pacing back and forth, holding a grocery bag. His girl friend, Jill, who works nearby, arrives, smiling. They kiss, settle down on a bench, and unpack the groceries to have lunch together. He is glum because he has been laid off, which means postponing their wedding plans, and he doesn't know how to tell her. While they sit, first an old lady and then a teenage boy pass them, moving away from the camera. Suddenly, the boy attacks the old lady and tries to grab her handbag. She struggles, screaming. Eddie jumps up and rushes over. The boy sees him coming and runs into a building, clutching the handbag. The scene will be continued later inside the building.

Take   1: Director: "Not bad. Eddie, tone down the nervousness. She mustn't suspect something right away." The prop man refills the grocery bag with fresh sandwiches and sodas.

Take   2: The DP is scanning the sky through his filter. A cloud is moving in, and the scene suddenly darkens. Light changes go unnoticed in real life but not on the screen.

Take   3: Jill fluffs a line and tries to improvise to save the take, but it doesn't quite work. The director insists on the exact wording.

Take   4: The teenager misses his mark, attacking the old lady before the assistant cameraman had time to adjust focus.

Take   5: A good one. The script supervisor looks at the stopwatch and says, "A minute and fifty." Director: "Too slow. Let's see if we can't tighten it up a bit."

Take   6: A fly settles on Eddie's sandwich as he is about to take a bite.

Take 7: Everything is going fine when an airplane is heard approaching. All eyes turn to the sound mixer. He shakes his head. The track is ruined.

Take 8: The teenager slips while running away, which would have given Eddie time to catch up with him.

Take 9: Very good. Jill: "Can I have one more, please. I feel I can do better."

Take 10: "Print. That's the one."

And if not, it goes to take eleven, and take twelve, and ... until it's right—or the sandwiches run out. That was a relatively simple scene; problems start multiplying when more action, more actors, children, or animals are involved.

Takes are usually no longer than two minutes, although a thousand-foot, 35-mm magazine can run for about eleven minutes. The second camera assistant keeps a constant watch on the amount of film remaining in the magazine, and when he sees that there is not enough left for another take, he announces, "Camera reloads," no matter how intense the pressure. It is a serious blunder to allow a good take to be spoiled because the film ran out. A top camera crew can remove the spent magazine, thread the new film through complex loops, test-run it, and be ready in thirty seconds, but even that time lag is an annoyance to actors and directors working at fever pitch, convinced that THE perfect take is just within their grasp. I once heard director Stuart Rosenberg mutter, only half in jest, "Why don't they invent an endless mag?"

A scene is seldom shot from one angle only. Usually it is split up into long shots, medium shots, and close-ups. The scene just described would be shot next from a reverse angle, called a "one-eighty." Many esoteric and colorful expressions are used in the industry: In a "three-sixty" the camera pans around full circle, and the entire crew has to go into hiding; "eighty-six" is a verb meaning "to remove," as in "eighty-six the ashtray"; a "Coney Island" is a sandbag, at least on the East Coast; "kill the brute" means "shut off the arc light"; the "window" is the last shot of the day; the "windowsill" is the one preceding it; and a "pick-up" is a small segment of a take to be reshot. When a scene is complete, but a new one is coming up on the same set, the expression is "F.D.R." (New Deal). And when every scene for a particular set is finished, and the crew is ready to move, the first assistant director announces, "Ladies and gentlemen, we are on the wrong set." Once, after finishing an exterior that took all morning, the first assistant said just that, and an extra, obviously new in the business, mumbled, "I don't understand these people. We have been shooting here for hours, and only now do they realize it was the wrong set!"

A major motion picture is a gigantic operation that consumes an inordinate amount of money day after day—

something like eight to ten thousand dollars an hour. The pressure is therefore enormous to get a scene ready and shot and to move on to the next one as quickly as possible. Yet, the rhythm of shooting is not that of constantly rolling cameras. It is more like a chart of ups and downs—peaks of high intensity followed by long breaks. When a scene has to be shot from a different angle it requires lengthy relighting and redressing. Actors use the time to relax with a game of cards or to go over the script in their dressing room. Extras form long lines at the public phones to check in with their answering services about another day's booking. Ironically, extras do not want to appear up front in crowd scenes too often. That would make them recognizable to frequent moviegoers and therefore less employable.

The shooting schedule of a major movie varies from ten weeks to a year or more. Some producers, pressed for time, have been known to shoot without a day off for three weeks at a stretch, be it because the location has to be vacated—or the star released—by a certain date, or because anticipated adverse weather would ruin everything. Such a grueling schedule gets the work done but takes a heavy toll from the crew and the cast—and also the budget. Strict SAG (Screen Actors Guild) and crew union rules quickly escalate salaries to double and triple their normal rates when stipulated rules governing rest and meal periods are violated.

Usually, however, working at or near home base is confined to a five-day week. On location, it's six days. And on the seventh day everybody—except the director—takes it easy. Actors, just like ordinary folks, explore the countryside, go fishing and golfing, or visit the town's museums and tourist spots—except for superstars in a star-crazy city like Rome, where Ava Gardner could not set foot outside her hotel. Wherever she went, day or night, she was followed by hordes of *paparazzi*, even going to and from work at the studio.

By the time an average movie is completed, perhaps 250,000 to 300,000 feet of film will have been shot. This will be edited to about 11,000 feet, the amount needed for an average two-hour show. The photograph on page 114 is a further illustration of the amount of work that goes into a movie and the disproportion between collective effort and resulting screen time.

It is now 4:30 A.M. We have been working since five in the afternoon and will continue until the arrival of daylight forces us to stop. Although scenes are often shot "day for night"—shot in daylight, but in a way that gives the impression of night—in this instance deserted streets were needed. This scene of *The Wanderers* takes place in 1963. In the early afternoon, armed with a police permit, the prop department had lined the street with cars of that year. As soon as it got dark, we first shot the two young men waiting in the street and the girl arriving in her car. Then the camera was mounted on the hood of the car to film them as they drive to a party. To get that shot, the head grip and a half-dozen of his men first applied large suction cups to the sides of the car. Then, on this foundation they built an elaborate scaffolding of wooden planks and interconnecting metal tubing, all held together by C clamps, nails, and gaffers' tape. This took almost an hour and a half. Once they were satisfied that the construction was rock-solid, the grips stepped aside, and the camera, sound, and electrical departments moved in. Following precise instructions from the DP, the grips mounted the 35-mm Arriflex and its sound blimp on the center of the hood, using the specific lens the DP had chosen and placing the camera at the exact height needed to frame the actors and a portion of the car above and below the windshield. Two small spotlights were mounted to the left and right of the camera, and electricians carried out the DP's orders to soften or sharpen the intensity and adjust the range of the beams. The DP adjusted his lights until all glass glare and reflection had been eliminated, the actors were evenly lit, and a balance with the existing light from the street-lamps had been achieved.

While this was going on, the camera operator and his assistants locked the camera in position, checked the focus and electrical connections, attached the film magazine, and tested the camera motor. Before rolling, the DP will give them the f-stop for this particular setup.

Under normal conditions, the camera crew mans the camera and the electricians control the lights, but in this case, with the car speeding through the streets, the actors have to do it all. A cable snakes from the camera and its battery to the scaffolding, then under the front door to Ken Wahl, the actor at the left. Heavy-duty batteries for the lights are stored in the car trunk, and the switch is also near Ken. John Friedrich, in the center, will operate the slate. Karen Allen will have enough to do driving the car while looking constantly into blinding lights. Under the dashboard and just out of camera range, microphones that will record the conversation have been installed by the sound mixer.

We are now ready to shoot. The makeup man dashes in and checks the shine on Karen's nose. The wardrobe lady reminds John that the top button of his shirt must remain closed, as it was in the previous scene. Assistants run up and down the street asking people to go inside. Orders crackle over portable radios, instructing policemen at strategic street corners to stop traffic; it wouldn't do to have a current-model car suddenly appear.

Cradling his Nagra while jackknifed under the rear seat is the six-foot five-inch sound man who will monitor the dialogue through his earphones and tape it. With him is the nearly six-foot director who cannot watch his actors perform, only listen to them. Standby ... ROLL! Ken switches on the lights, then the camera. John lifts the slate, clearly calls out scene and take numbers, and brings the stick down sharply. They're off. They will go around the block, down several streets, and come back to this point in about five minutes.

This is the second time tonight that we have gone through the whole intricate set of preparations. Everything was ready several hours earlier, and a take had already been filmed when it was discovered that as the car was moving, the streetlights were projecting the shadow of the camera onto the hood. The entire scaffolding had to be dismantled and rebuilt at a lower elevation. At midnight we broke for a one-hour dinner. As we wait for the car to return, the tired among us try to catch a quick nap or scan the sky for that liberating first glimpse of blue.

In the photograph, the eerie-looking contraption coming down the street is nearing the end of its run. As soon as it stops, fifty hands, waiting just behind me, will pounce on it. The script man will record the amount of footage shot; the camera crew will reload; electricians will check lights, connecting cables, and batteries; grips will tighten clamps; prop people will clean the windshield. The director and the sound man will stretch their legs, and everyone will try to read the director. Is he happy? No, we go again.

The scene is shot seven more times before the director says "We're done. Print five and eight," and the first assistant yells the magic words: "It's a wrap." As we stash our gear away, production assistants run around collecting from all departments written reports of the scene just shot and handing out a call sheet to every crew member. This is our daily Bible, a work plan listing tomorrow's schedule in infinite detail: date; shooting-day numeral; scene numbers; how many pages of dialogue; names of the actors required and of the characters they play; when, where, and by whom the actors will be picked up, at what time they have to be made up, to be dressed, to be ready on the set; how many extras will be needed and where they are to assemble; how much coffee, doughnuts, etc. is to be available at what time on the set; the exact time each crew member is to report for work; instructions—and sometimes maps—on how to reach the location; and, finally, any special equipment, props, effects, wardrobe, hair, or makeup that will be needed.

Maybe two minutes of this night's work will end up on the screen. Bleary-eyed, we go home to crawl into bed at 7:00 A.M. The call is for 4:30 tomorrow afternoon. Another night's work. Another two minutes of the movie.

A Chorus Line (1986). The camera is ready, the dancers are ready. One last bit of emphatic direction from Sir Richard Attenborough

LEFT *Just Tell Me What You Want*
(1980). In Bergdorf Goodman, Alan
King has been knocked down by Ali
MacGraw. Actually, he is in pain from a
blow that landed harder than intended.
Sidney Lumet intently lives the scene.

OPPOSITE *The Rose* (1979). Director
Mark Rydell and DP Vilmos Zsigmond
follow a scene being shot in a Manhattan
street.

OPPOSITE   *The Fixer* (1968). Director John Frankenheimer *(in white pants)* and crew get out of the way as camera and arc light on dolly tracks are pushed back at full speed, just ahead of the running Alan Bates.

ABOVE   *Jaws* (1975). Teamsters drive the crew to the set at daybreak and back to the hotel at sunset. In between they may have many errands to run for the production—or none at all.

The Wanderers (1979). A tracking shot at a busy intersection of the Bronx, New York. The Baldies are leading away some defeated members of the Wanderers gang.

Moscow on the Hudson (1984). A running dolly shot on an interior set—a section of Bloomingdale's department store, reconstructed on a New York sound stage. The camera is racing at full speed just ahead of actor Robin Williams.

LEFT AND OPPOSITE *Lilith* (1964).
Warren Beatty and Jean Seberg. The
scene was shot the day before, but doubt
arose as to where Beatty's hand had been
when the scene was interrupted. An
urgent call brought the editor, Aram
Avakian, who now checks the take, frame
by frame. Director Robert Rossen, cast,
and crew wait with varying degrees of
impatience until the exact position is
determined.

LEFT *The Miracle Worker* (1962). Patty Duke and producer Fred Coe. A blanket wards off the early morning chill.

OPPOSITE *Deathtrap* (1982). Michael Caine offers his tea to Irene Worth during a tedious wait for camera and light adjustments on location.

ABOVE *The Bible* (1965). John Huston rehearsing with Richard Harris, who plays Cain, inside the crater of Mount Vesuvius formed by the eruption that buried Pompeii; the slope at left is the result of more recent eruptions.

OPPOSITE *The Bible* (1965). Inside the crater of Mount Vesuvius, John Huston shows Richard Harris how to act out the agony of Cain's banishment into the wilderness.

The Fixer (1968). Shooting in a crowded peasant hut in Hungary. Writer Dalton Trumbo is seated at the table *(center)*; John Frankenheimer, torso bared, stands by the camera; Alan Bates is at right.

The Pope of Greenwich Village (1984). Director Stuart Rosenberg *(second from left)* shoots a scene in a dance class. DP John Bailey kneels by the camera. At left, first assistant director Joe Napolitano

ABOVE   *The Cardinal* (1963). Romy Schneider, wearing the tea cozy as a cardinal's hat, shows her enthusiasm for a 6:30 A.M. breakfast call.

OPPOSITE   *Klute* (1971). Donald Sutherland and Jane Fonda relax on a sofa between takes. A mirror in the ceiling plays tricks with his face.

Tom Jones (1963). The camera records what it feels like to have the point of a sword aimed between the eyes.
Camera and operator are dragged across the forest floor on a blanket. Director Tony Richardson is at left, standing.

An Unmarried Woman (1977). Panaglide cameraman, running up the steps behind Jill Clayburgh, can film such scenes without camera-shake.

Doctor Dolittle (1967). On a beach in
Santa Lucia, a chimp is curious about
Samantha Eggar's dress, looks under it,
and swoons.

The Wanderers (1979). This weird contraption is a car rigged to record the scene independently while the actors drive and talk.

Sooner or Later (1979). Sawing off the front of the car allows better camera angles on Denise Miller and Rex Smith. The steering wheel is held in place by sandbags. The camera operator is Peter Garbarini.

OPPOSITE *Moscow on the Hudson* (1984). Director Paul Mazursky mimics the musician who had played together with Robin Williams earlier but then had to leave. Now the camera is recording the reactions of jazz club patrons.

ABOVE *A Man Could Get Killed* (1966). Between takes on a luxury yacht, Melina Mercouri teaches steps of the Hassapiko to co-star James Garner.

Just Tell Me What You Want (1980). Director Sidney Lumet rehearsing with Ali MacGraw. When shown this photograph, Lumet said he would title it "Don't bother wrapping it up."

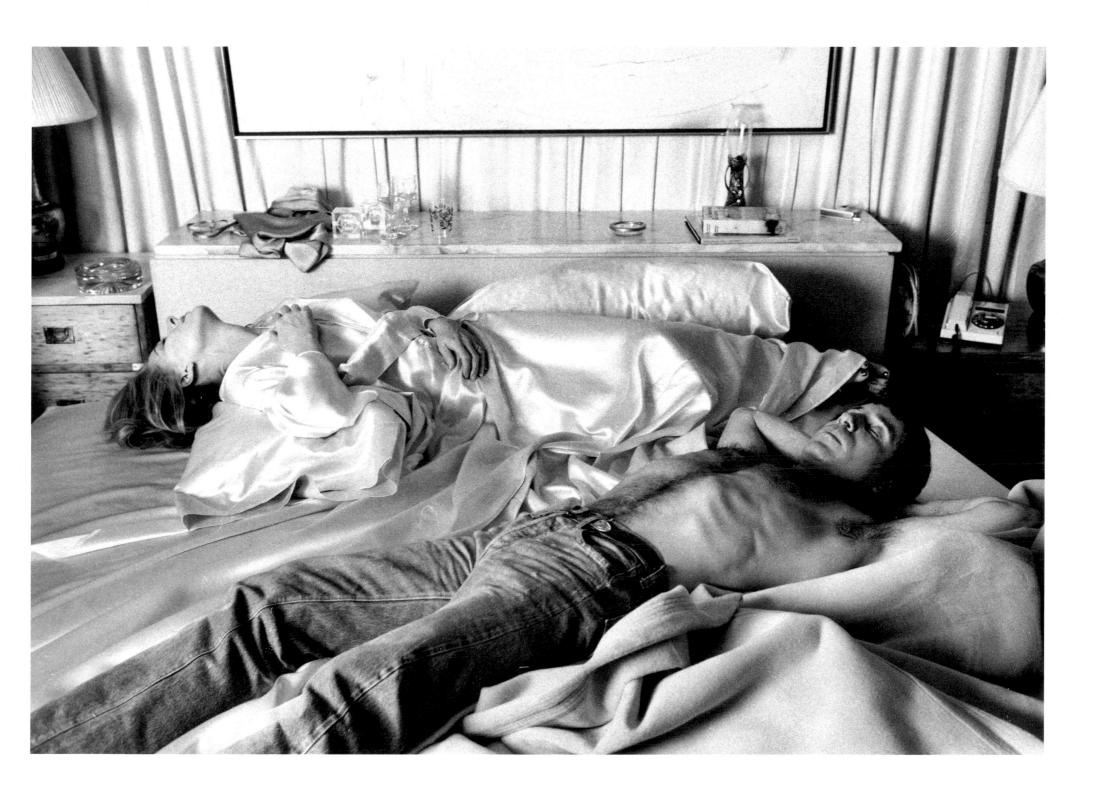

One-Trick Pony (1980). Joan Hackett and Paul Simon take a quick nap on the set, waiting for lights to be adjusted.

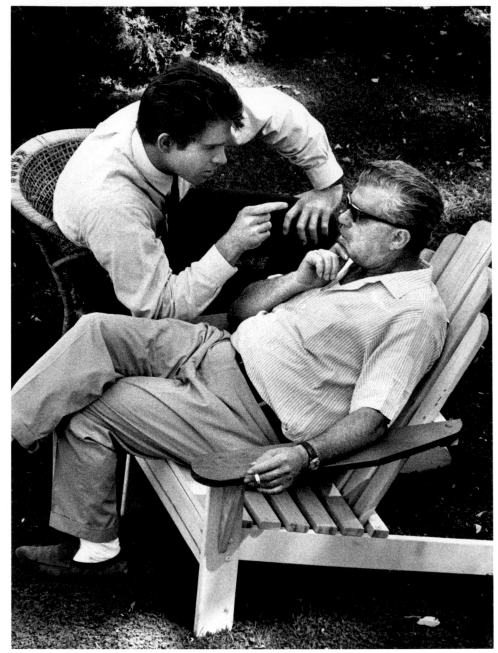

ABOVE LEFT   *Lilith* (1964). Director Robert Rossen and Jean Seberg

ABOVE RIGHT   *Lilith* (1964). Artistic differences between Warren Beatty and director Robert Rossen were hashed out in frequent *tête-à-têtes*. This picture was taken from a safe distance.

OPPOSITE   *Girl with Green Eyes* (1964). Peter Finch and director Desmond Davis working out a problem on location in Ireland.

Blow Out (1981). The black panel will eliminate reflections as the camera circles John Lithgow in the telephone booth. Director Brian De Palma has to follow the action on his knees.

An Unmarried Woman (1977). For the difficult scene in which Michael Murphy breaks down and admits his infidelity to Jill Clayburgh, the crew and director Paul Mazursky (black hat) hit the pavement to avoid eye contact. Only the first assistant director (Terry Donnelly) remains standing behind the camera operator (Lou Barlia) to check on background traffic and extras.

OPPOSITE *Tom Jones* (1963). Susannah York, Tony Richardson, and Albert Finney return singing from a scene improvised in torrential rain.

ABOVE *Tom Jones* (1963). Susannah York, in a beautiful eighteenth-century gown, is ready. While final preparations are carried out, director Tony Richardson thinks about the scene or catches a quick nap. It's hard to tell.

OPPOSITE *Blow Out* (1981). DP Vilmos Zsigmond steadies John Travolta's hand for screen-filling close-ups of evidence found in a murder inquiry. The operator is Jan Keisser.

ABOVE *Blow Out* (1981). DP Vilmos Zsigmond moves Nancy Allen in step with the camera as it follows John Travolta, pacing back and forth (*unseen at left*), in dialogue with her. Michael Gershman is maintaining focus.

OPPOSITE *Jaws* (1975). Out at sea, Richard Dreyfuss enjoys a good joke, a welcome relief during a long day of difficult takes in dangerous waters.

ABOVE *Just Tell Me What You Want* (1980). In the bedroom scene, the dialogue between Ali MacGraw and Peter Weller *(right)* was serious. Alan King, not part of the scene but standing nearby, jumped into bed to liven things up and wound up holding hands with Weller.

LEFT *Sinful Davey* (1968). John Huston working out the moves of a duel.

OPPOSITE *Tom Jones* (1963). Albert Finney, in rehearsal, about to deliver the decisive blow. He will, however, smash the sword into the ground.

OPPOSITE   *Alfred the Great* (1969). Irish troops train for Viking battle scenes.

ABOVE   *Tom Jones* (1963). Director Tony Richardson stages a fight in a cemetery, using art department human bones as weapons.

Exodus (1960). Paul Newman and Otto Preminger, just before shooting a scene at dawn in an Arab village.

The Verdict (1982). Sidney Lumet rehearsing with Paul Newman on location in Boston.

OPPOSITE *What's New Pussycat?* (1965). Paris resident Romy Schneider takes Paula Prentiss, Peter O'Toole, and his children to the Marché aux Puces on a day off from shooting.

ABOVE *The Fixer* (1968). Carol White, fresh in from London and wearing a miniskirt, created quite a sensation in the streets of Budapest.

ABOVE *Jaws* (1975). Robert Shaw, on bridge, hooked a harpoon into the shark, who then dived and came up exactly in front of the camera in its waterproof casing. After many unsuccessful tries, the scene finally works, with beautiful precision.

OPPOSITE *Moscow on the Hudson* (1984). Maria Conchita, off-camera, vents her anger at Robin Williams *(being filmed unseen at left)* in words and gestures—with a strong assist from director Paul Mazursky.

LEFT   *Jaws* (1975). Moviemaking
creates strange situations. An invisible
platform makes it appear as though the
crew is walking on water.

OPPOSITE, ABOVE AND BELOW   *Jaws*
(1975). Robert Shaw is about to be
devoured by the shark. Cut. Print.
Lunch, one hour.

OPPOSITE   *Alfred the Great* (1969). David Hemmings *(third from left)* brought his Rolls-Royce to the battlefield and gets admiring comments from fellow actors.

ABOVE LEFT   *The Miracle Worker* (1962). Patty Duke takes care of her pet kitten during a lunch-hour break.

ABOVE RIGHT   *Tom Jones* (1963). David Warner, in eighteenth-century finery and modern rain bonnet, fills the time between takes with a soccer ball.

LEFT   *Prince of the City* (1981). A mobster, played by Ron Maccone, will be found dead in a garbage can. Director Sidney Lumet applies finishing touches while propmasters J. Oates and J. Caracciolo wait to drop the can in front of the camera lens, at street-level.

OPPOSITE   *Tom Jones* (1963). Director Tony Richardson shows spectator at public-hanging scene how to display her pet.

The Turning Point (1977). Two cameras record American Ballet Theatre dancers, coming out of the wings at full speed.

The Turning Point (1977). Dancers relaxing between takes.

OPPOSITE *Klute* (1971). A lot of time is spent in waiting. Technicians and the producer *(foreground)* are catching up with the news while director Alan J. Pakula and Jane Fonda rehearse in an apartment upstairs.

ABOVE *Blow Out* (1981). Nancy Allen, Brian De Palma, and John Travolta, waiting on the set for adjustments to be completed, concentrate on the upcoming scene.

All the President's Men (1976). Alan J. Pakula rehearsing with Robert Redford in a real Washington, D.C., courtroom

The Cardinal (1963). Otto Preminger shows Tom Tryon and Romy Schneider how he wants fear expressed in the scene.

FAR LEFT *Tom Jones* (1963). Coming out of the forest after a day's shooting, Albert Finney clowns on the way back to his car.

LEFT *Tom Jones* (1963). Tony Richardson watches as Susannah York and Albert Finney rehearse minuet steps in eighteenth-century costumes. Plastic bonnets protect them against a gentle drizzle. The location is Somerset, England.

ABOVE *The Turning Point* (1977). Herbert Ross directing Leslie Browne.

ABOVE *The Miracle Worker* (1962). Patty Duke and Anne Bancroft engage in a bit of horseplay between takes of an emotionally difficult scene.

OPPOSITE *The Miracle Worker* (1962). Crates of chicken eggs ready to hatch were standing by for the scene in which Anne Bancroft teaches Patty Duke, as the young Helen Keller, the mystery of birth. Director Arthur Penn places a hatching egg in Patty's hand just before camera rolls.

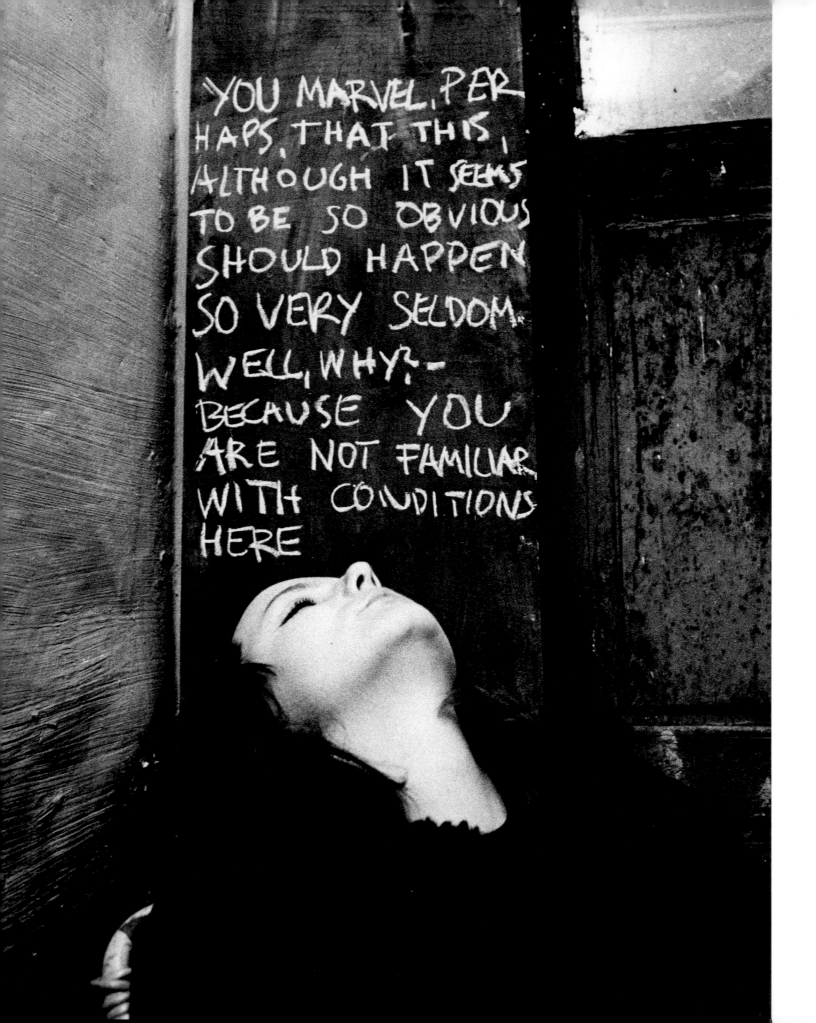

YOU MARVEL, PER
HAPS, THAT THIS,
ALTHOUGH IT SEEMS
TO BE SO OBVIOUS
SHOULD HAPPEN
SO VERY SELDOM.
WELL, WHY? —
BECAUSE YOU
ARE NOT FAMILIAR
WITH CONDITIONS
HERE

LEFT *The Castle* (1968). Another
strange real-life situation on a movie set.
Prompting panels were used to help the
German-speaking actors. The script girl
fell asleep between camera setups near
one such panel, creating a moment of
Kafka-within-Kafka.

OPPOSITE *The Turning Point* (1977).
Wherever one looked on that set there
were little Degas tableaux.

LEFT *Sooner or Later* (1979). Rex Smith and Denise Miller, a young couple in love, stand on a revolving platform. The camera, on a wheelchair, will circle around them along the taped outline, creating the impression of a spinning room. The man at lower right regulates the platform's speed, and the director, Bruce Hart, with nowhere to stand, will watch the action from flat on his back.

OPPOSITE *Tom Jones* (1963). Susannah York, in eighteenth-century dress, plays with her dog between takes.

ABOVE *One-Trick Pony* (1980). Paul Simon starred and wrote the script. In this bedroom scene, the dialogue didn't feel right. While Blair Brown, camera, and crew wait, he rewrites it.

OPPOSITE *The Alamo* (1960). John Wayne, who directed the movie and also starred in it, shows a Mexican woman how she should grieve for a fallen son. The full-scale replica of the fort, built on a Texas ranch near Brackettville, is in the background.

LEFT   *The Alamo* (1960). With a touch of elegance, Laurence Harvey, like his character, Colonel Travis, the only Englishman among the defenders, soaks up the Texas sun between takes.

RIGHT   *The Bible* (1965). Peter O'Toole, as the Angel Messenger of God, enjoys a cigarette between takes.

162

LEFT   *The Alamo* (1960). Richard Boone intently follows a rehearsal.

RIGHT   *Alfred the Great* (1969). David Hemmings as King Alfred takes a break between difficult shots of the deposed king wading in a river.

Tom Jones (1963). Crew and extras wait for director Tony Richardson to think out the blocking of a scene in a cemetery.

ABOVE *Blow Out* (1981). To get a scene ready takes time. Director Brian De Palma, shooting in Philadelphia's main railroad station, has no choice but to wait. Onlookers and passengers are kept out of the way.

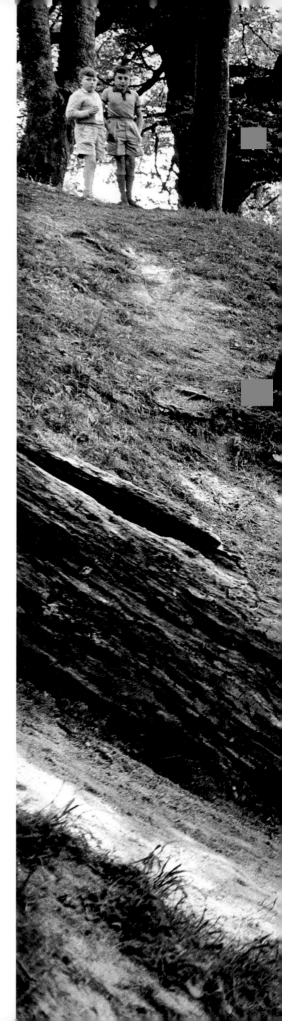

ABOVE   *The Verdict* (1982). In this scene, Paul Newman has just slapped
Charlotte Rampling to the ground in the bar of a hotel. While the lights are
being adjusted for another take, each remained in position, deep in
thought.

OPPOSITE   *Tom Jones* (1963). Albert Finney has isolated himself while a
forest scene is being readied. Two boys, at top left, watch cautiously.

A Walk with Love and Death (1969). The camera rolls and the slate, with all pertinent information and gray-scale, is about to be marked. Principals are Anjelica Huston, daughter of John Huston, and Assaf Dayan, son of Moshe Dayan.

ACTORS ACTING

Actors in motion pictures are subject to the same frustrations that affect the director; everything is done in little bits and pieces and in no chronological order.

Because of the particular conditions created by weather and the availability of actors, sets, or props, a take that is shot in the afternoon may have no relation whatsoever in time or place to one shot that same morning, and it may be part of a scene that was started several weeks ago, to be completed several weeks later. In this gigantic jigsaw puzzle, only the director knows where and how each isolated piece will fit with the ones preceding and following it.

In the theater an actor can soar for a sustained period, with the essential awareness of continuity, and along the way draw on the very tangible vibrations emanating from a live audience.

In a movie, by contrast, he is given footage for a minute or two at a time, during which he has to act out of context, before a frigid camera lens, under hot, blinding lights, surrounded by a maze of equipment, and constantly under the merciless scrutiny of technicians watching his every twitch from just a few feet away.

True, a scene is usually first shot in its entirety from one point of view, without interruption. This is called the master take, but it is not the one you will see. The master shows everything and is occasionally used in editing, but that's all. To prevent the audience from getting visually restless and to foster deeper spectator involvement, small segments of that scene are then shot again with different lenses and from various angles, all of which is called "coverage." And each time, with the dialogue now narrowed down to just a few lines, the actor has to repeat the same gestures and inflections and is expected to match the "feel" of all the other takes, so that when the different angles are later intercut, the result will be one homogenous flow. A tough proposition.

Moreover, these shots are not done in one continuous wave. A "one-eighty" may entail the addition of walls and extensive set redressing, which means an hour or more of idle time for the actor, who then has to rev himself up again to proper pitch. No wonder, then, that it is nearly impossible, even for an experienced actor, to evaluate the totality of his performance. It will be revealed only later, when the editing is done. In the meantime, there is much insecurity, and actors must rely on the director's judgment to guide them.

It also takes extraordinary concentration to be able to ignore the various activities that must be carried out by the crew during the actual shooting. Some actors, either by training or inborn talent, can so absorb themselves in their roles that on "Action" the rest of the world disappears. I can be aiming my camera at their faces from three feet away, but they don't see me. Conversely, other actors are thrown off by the slightest distraction, even by so minute an item as a technician's bright shirt. The first thing such an actor will ask is that everybody get out of his line of vision. If that isn't enough, the director will order anyone not essential to the scene to leave the set altogether. The crew take it in stride; it's all part of a day's work. Nothing much fazes them. There are times, however, when a scene works so well and an actor's performance is so galvanizing that on "Cut," the crew will spontaneously burst into applause. This kind of reaction from the blasé troops is the ultimate accolade.

One fringe benefit of the business is the opportunity to witness great acting frequently, and great acting is not necessarily the exclusive province of the famous actors or the stars. Most actors are not famous, and many of them are total unknowns who may come through in small roles with wonderful performances that are a thrill to watch. Undeniably, to work closely with a star adds a certain excitement to which one never becomes fully immune. What is it like to work with a star on a day-to-day basis?

Although their every whim is catered to, the stars reserve the glamour for their private lives. On the set it's strictly business and they work hard, just like everybody else. A 6 A.M. makeup call does not suggest pampered treatment. On the surface, an air of professionalism pervades every aspect of the job. The tone is "we're all in this together," and when things go well everything is fine. There is a warm and friendly relationship with the crew, and a sense of cooperation that makes every task easier. But it is different when things do not go well, and a star can be testy for any number of reasons: He may disagree with the director's concept but not get his way; the female lead may have started the picture with high hopes but is rebelling now because she feels it is going downhill; he may have preferred other co-actors; she doesn't like her close-ups in yesterday's love scene and wants them reshot softer; he wasn't crazy about the movie or his part from the beginning, but took it because he hadn't worked for a while or was under contract to do it; he may feel he could have negotiated a better deal. None of this, in a star's view, would be called being difficult; it is rather "standing up for what you know is right." Petty upstaging rivalries and jealousies also come to the fore when a co-star gets more close-ups, an enlarged role, or more press coverage. Deeply seated personal dislikes can turn the set into a snakepit. And finally, some stars believe that making demands adds to their stature.

"Being difficult" can be expressed in obvious or subtle—but always unmistakable—ways. The star is not on time, and time lost on a production is very costly; he is too tired for rehearsals after the day's shooting; the dressing room is too far from the set; the lunch the company serves is lousy so he drives, or has to be driven, to a distant restaurant, and this affects the afternoon shooting schedule; he will do nothing to help his co-actors in their performances, and so on. The variations are endless, depending on personal style. I suppose the ultimate way of expressing displeasure—and establishing status—is to get someone fired. It goes without saying that only a superstar can hope to get away with such behavior for any length of time. Inflated egos and unacceptable deportment from actors of lesser stature will not be tolerated.

The prevailing mood on a set is seldom happy and relaxed. An air of high-voltage intensity is common, and there is no such thing as a movie without a crisis. Eeny, meeny, miney, mo ... Okay, *Lilith*: The story deals with a young drifter, played by Warren Beatty, who takes a job at a mental institution and is drawn into the psychotic world of a beautiful inmate (Jean Seberg). Peter Fonda plays the role of a fellow inmate; he too is in love with the girl.

The picture was shot entirely on location. An imposing mansion on a Long Island estate that once belonged to a United States ambassador served as the institution. Other exteriors were shot in Maryland. The estate was of magnificent proportions: A long, tree-lined driveway led to the mansion, from which perfectly manicured lawns fanned out; shaded garden walks and flower beds surrounded an elegant circular fountain. There was also, of course, a full-size swimming pool, and a silvery stream meandered through a very pretty wooded area. In this idyllic setting it should have been a "happy" picture, but it was not.

The problems that beset the making of *Lilith* were of a personal nature. The director was Robert Rossen, a well-established name with pictures such as *They Came to Cordura*, *Body and Soul*, and *The Hustler* to his credit. But this time, he was a sick man; his whole body was covered with eczema. He would direct in the stifling heat, scratching himself incessantly wherever his hands could reach, constantly reopening old sores. He would go through six brand-new T-shirts every day. The drugs and antibiotics he took did not relieve the eczema, but they made him drowsy and sapped his energy.

To cope with the exhausting demands of his job, a director has to remain in top form, physically and mentally.

In this weakened condition Robert Rossen had to direct a Warren Beatty who, on this picture, was particularly difficult. In every scene he argued doggedly with Rossen about one point or another. Moreover, there were personality clashes between Beatty and Fonda. They just did not get along. This combination of factors created an atmosphere that was perpetually heavy with tension. I do not know why Beatty was difficult. I was not part of his "inner circle," and his attitude may well have been justified. Ultimately I did get the shots and special setups that were needed, but I always had a knot in my stomach when I approached Beatty, fearful that I had misjudged his "cooperation index" of the moment.

Several weeks after the picture wrapped, to my great surprise Warren called me at home one day. He said he knew he had not been easy to work with; he hinted at great pressures from all sides and suggested that we meet socially. It was his way of saying he was sorry, and I greatly appreciated the gesture. We saw a movie together, munching on sandwiches. Then he showed me around that part of Manhattan where he and his sister, Shirley MacLaine, lived when they were starting their careers. He even gave me an impromptu acting lesson at a street corner. "Now look what you can do with a simple sentence like 'The light is changing,'" he said. "It all depends on where you put the inflection."

THE light is changing. (There is only one.)

The LIGHT is changing. (And nothing else.)

The light IS changing. (There had been doubt.)

The light is CHANGING. (It was unexpected.)

Later, he took me along on a visit to the playwright Eugene Ionesco, and we wound up the evening in a restaurant, joining a party of his show-business friends.

All evening long, *Lilith* was not mentioned even once.

It would be wrong, however, to assume that a star's presence is necessarily a cause of trouble. Even when the stars are absolute pussycats, problems of one kind or another are certain to pop up. The production is behind schedule or over budget and the studio is complaining; the costume designer had it out with the production manager and quit; the writer has been barred from the set; the DP is about to be replaced. With the exception of an occasional volcanic outburst in front of the crew, these conflicts are usually played out away from the set, but they are palpable nevertheless.

A cynical remark sums up how crises are dealt with: "Search for the guilty, punish the innocent, promote the incompetent." Never a dull moment.

One-Trick Pony (1980). Paul Simon,
performing, also wrote the script.

The World of Henry Orient (1964). Peter Sellers as the sexually obsessed concert pianist

The Verdict (1982). Paul Newman lost none of his intensity between takes of the courtroom scenes.

The Dealing (1972). John Lithgow and Robert Lyons, a spirited team

Blow Out (1981). John Lithgow as the ice-pick killer

LEFT *The Chairman* (1969).
Gregory Peck is caught in a
demonstration by the Red Guards
during China's Cultural Revolution.
The scene was shot on a back lot at the
Shepperton Studios in England.

OPPOSITE *The Fixer* (1968). Alan Bates
runs for cover during a pogrom in Kiev.
The scene was shot in the old ghetto of
Budapest.

Jaws (1975). In the chilling opening scene, an elaborate system of ropes and pulleys, anchored under the sea, was used to create the effect of a girl being mauled by a shark.

The Pope of Greenwich Village (1984). Eric Roberts gets his thumb cut off as punishment for having stolen Mafia money.

The Wanderers (1979). During a fight between rival gangs on a football field, the father of a Wanderer
(Bud Andrews) steps in to lend a hand.

Just Tell Me What You Want (1980). Ali MacGraw has cornered her double-dealing lover, Alan King, in Bergdorf Goodman, an elegant New York department store, and knocked him to the ground. The scene was shot in the store on a Sunday.

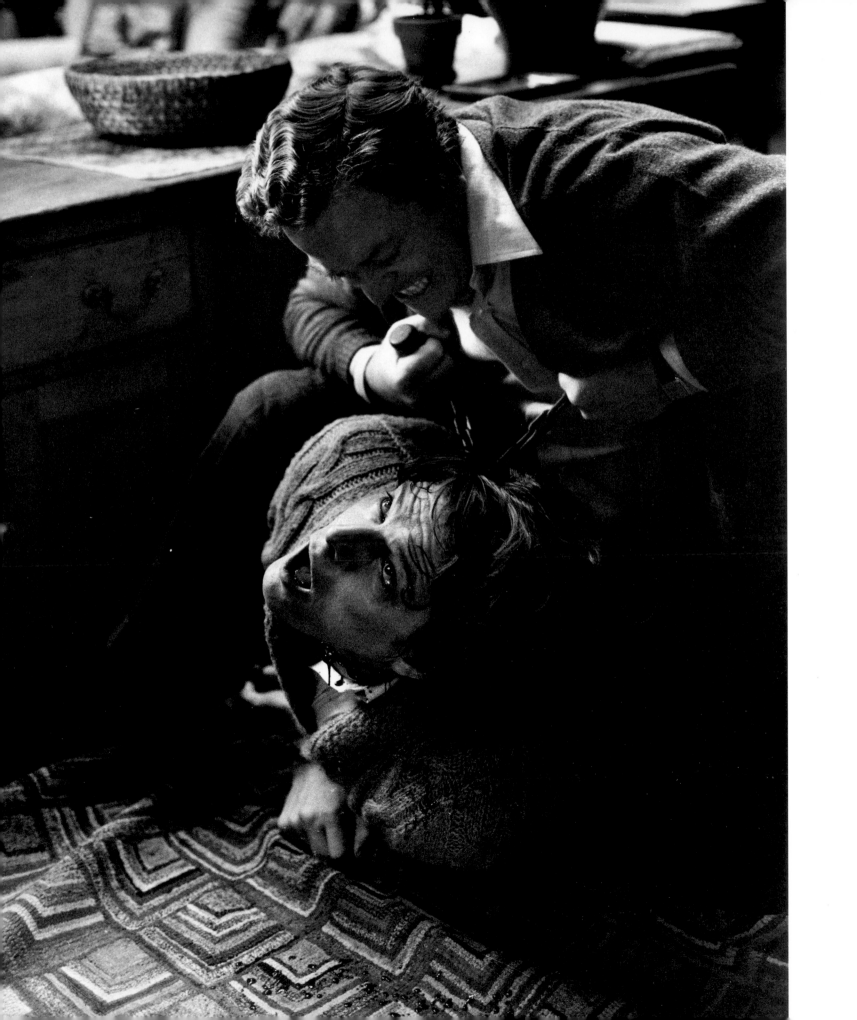

OPPOSITE *Deathtrap* (1982). Michael Caine strangles Christopher Reeve. The fake blood comes from a tube, cleverly hidden behind the chain and activated by remote control.

ABOVE *Tom Jones* (1963). Diane Cilento and Albert Finney

LEFT *What's New Pussycat?* (1965).
Peter O'Toole brings flowers to Romy
Schneider.

OPPOSITE *Moscow on the Hudson*
(1984). Robin Williams hides from
pursuing KGB officials—"behind" a
Bloomingdale's salesgirl.

OPPOSITE   *The Castle* (1968). Much of the movie was shot in a small Austrian village near Graz. This local farmer was hired for his face—as is.

ABOVE   *The Flim-Flam Man* (1967). George C. Scott in the title role.

Ulysses (1967). Milo O'Shea and Barbara Jefford, as Leopold and Molly Bloom, in the only happy recollection in her monologue, of the time they went a-courting.

The Wanderers (1979). Ken Wahl and John Friedrich are winning the strip poker game easily—by cheating
Tony Kalem and Karen Allen *(right)*.

What's New Pussycat? (1965). Woody Allen acted in this movie, which he wrote the script for but did not direct.
Waiting for him is German actress Catherine Shaake.

Ulysses (1967). Barbara Jefford, as Molly Bloom, can't quite get used to the way her husband, Leopold, likes to sleep.

LEFT *What's New Pussycat?* (1965). Ursula Andress

OPPOSITE *Moscow on the Hudson* (1984). Robin Williams as the Russian circus musician who defects while visiting New York and finds that life in the land of freedom is not without its problems.

An Unmarried Woman (1977). Jill Clayburgh, in her apartment, briefly fancies herself as a ballet dancer.

Klute (1971). Jane Fonda has a last look at her empty apartment before starting a new life with Donald Sutherland.

ABOVE   *Modesty Blaise* (1966). Monica Vitti as the seductive private eye

OPPOSITE   *What's New Pussycat?* (1965). Paula Prentiss in a striptease scene

OPPOSITE   *The Castle* (1968). Maximilian Schell as the depressed main character, caught in the quicksand of a faceless bureaucracy

ABOVE   *Lilith* (1964). Warren Beatty and Jean Seberg starred in the story of a young man who takes a job as a therapist trainee at a mental institution and then is drawn into the strange world of a beautiful inmate.

LEFT *Thieves* (1977). Could that be
director Bob Fosse behind those Fosse
Grants? It is, playing a Bowery bum.

OPPOSITE *Star!* (1968). Julie Andrews
as Gertrude Lawrence arriving in New York.

OPPOSITE *What's New Pussycat?* (1965). Peter Sellers and Peter O'Toole, both drunk, harmonize in a Paris bistro.

ABOVE *All the President's Men* (1976). During rehearsal, Robert Redford fluffs a line and Dustin Hoffman chides him with an expletive that is becoming less and less unprintable.

205

ABOVE *Billy Jack Goes to Washington* (1976). Tom Laughlin, director and star, confronts
E. G. Marshall with a stack of fake cables. An expensive movie that required a full-scale
reconstruction of the Senate chamber, it was completed but never released.

OPPOSITE *The Miracle Worker* (1962). The climactic moment when, having taught the young
Helen Keller (Patty Duke), how to communicate with other human beings, Anne Bancroft
hands her over to her family.

OPPOSITE   *The Bible* (1965). George C. Scott, as Abraham, pleading with
God to spare Sodom and Gomorrah. Each morning, it took hours to
reapply his beard.

ABOVE   *The Young Doctors* (1961). Fredric March in the role of a chief
pathologist

The Hill (1965). Sean Connery is one of the soldiers undergoing cruel punishment in a British Army stockade.

The Alamo (1960). The defenders are lining up in front of the fort, a full-scale reconstruction on a Texas ranch. In front, Richard Widmark, Laurence Harvey, and John Wayne, who directed the movie.

211

PARTING SHOT

Despite crises, blunders, tantrums, and reshoots, the day comes when the last take is in the can and the movie wraps.

It may become a smash hit, or it may never recover its cost. There is just no way of predicting how good or bad a movie will be, or how it will be received by the critics and the public. There is no sure formula for success.

Splice two pieces of film together and something magical may ignite the screen—or may not. Superstars, mega-budgets, famous directors, wall-to-wall screens, and best-sellers are no guarantee. I have worked on movies that won Oscars, but at the time I had no idea that the film would be acclaimed. Sometimes I was sure that a film would reap every trophy, but then it opened and left town in a week.

At least you now have an inkling of what goes into the little stub that you throw away as you take your seat and feel a tingle of anticipated excitement when the houselights dim.

Everyone involved has done his very best.

I hope it's a good one.

FILMOGRAPHY

FILM TITLE	DIRECTOR	PRINCIPAL ACTORS
1. The Alamo (1960)	John Wayne	John Wayne, Richard Widmark, Laurence Harvey, Richard Boone
2. Exodus (1960)	Otto Preminger	Paul Newman, Eva Marie Saint
3. The Young Doctors (1961)	Phil Karlson	Fredric March, Ben Gazzara, Ina Balin
4. Requiem for a Heavyweight (1962)	Ralph Nelson	Anthony Quinn, Jackie Gleason, Mickey Rooney, Julie Harris
5. Judgment at Nuremberg (1962)	Stanley Kramer	Spencer Tracy, Marlene Dietrich, Burt Lancaster, Maximilian Schell, Richard Widmark, Judy Garland
6. The Miracle Worker (1962)	Arthur Penn	Patty Duke, Anne Bancroft
7. Love Is a Ball (1962)	David Swift	Glenn Ford, Charles Boyer, Hope Lange
8. Tom Jones (1963)	Tony Richardson	Albert Finney, Susannah York
9. The Running Man (1963)	Sir Carol Reed	Laurence Harvey, Alan Bates, Lee Remick
10. The Cardinal (1963)	Otto Preminger	Tom Tryon, Carol Lynley, Romy Schneider
11. Girl with Green Eyes (1964)	Desmond Davis	Peter Finch, Rita Tushingham, Lynn Redgrave
12. Lilith (1964)	Robert Rossen	Warren Beatty, Jean Seberg, Peter Fonda
13. The World of Henry Orient (1964)	George Roy Hill	Peter Sellers, Tippy Walker, Merri Spaeth, Paula Prentiss
14. The Bible (1965)	John Huston	George C. Scott, Ava Gardner, Peter O'Toole, John Huston
15. The Hill (1965)	Sidney Lumet	Sean Connery, Ossie Davis
16. What's New Pussycat? (1965)	Clive Donner	Peter O'Toole, Peter Sellers, Woody Allen, Ursula Andress, Romy Schneider
17. A Man Could Get Killed (1966)	Cliff Owen; Ronald Neame	Melina Mercouri, James Garner
18. Modesty Blaise (1966)	Joseph Losey	Monica Vitti, Dirk Bogarde, Terence Stamp
19. The Honey Pot (1966)	Joseph L. Mankiewicz	Rex Harrison, Susan Hayward, Maggie Smith, Cliff Robertson, Capucine, Edie Adams

20. The Bells of Hell (Not completed)	David Miller	Gregory Peck
21. Ulysses (1967)	Joseph Strick	Milo O'Shea, Barbara Jefford, Maurice Roeves
22. The Flim-Flam Man (1967)	Irvin Kershner	George C. Scott, Michael Sarrazin, Sue Lyon
23. Doctor Dolittle (1967)	Richard Fleischer	Rex Harrison, Anthony Newley, Samantha Eggar, Richard Attenborough
24. Valley of the Dolls (1967)	Mark Robson	Barbara Parkins, Paul Burke, Patty Duke, Susan Hayward, Sharon Tate
25. Star! (1968)	Robert Wise	Julie Andrews, Richard Crenna, Daniel Massey
26. Sinful Davey (1968)	John Huston	John Hurt, Pamela Franklin
27. Inspector Clouseau (1968)	Bud Yorkin	Alan Arkin, Delia Boccardo
28. Decline and Fall (1968)	John Kirsh	Robin Phillips, Genevieve Page
29. The Fixer (1968)	John Frankenheimer	Alan Bates, Dirk Bogarde
30. The Castle (1968)	Rudolph Noelte	Maximilian Schell
31. Hannibal Brooks (1968)	Michael Winner	Oliver Reed, Michael J. Pollard
32. Popi (1969)	Arthur Hiller	Alan Arkin, Rita Moreno
33. Alfred the Great (1969)	Clive Donner	David Hemmings, Michael York
34. 100 Rifles (1969)	Tom Gries	Jim Brown, Raquel Welch
35. A Walk with Love and Death (1969)	John Huston	Assaf Dayan, Anjelica Huston
36. The Chairman (1969)	J. Lee-Thompson	Gregory Peck, Anne Heywood
37. Change of Mind (1969)	Robert Stevens	Raymond St. Jacques, Susan Oliver
38. Move (1970)	Stuart Rosenberg	Elliott Gould
39. Tropic of Cancer (1970)	Joseph Strick	Rip Torn
40. Madron (1970)	Jerry Hopper	Richard Boone, Leslie Caron
41. Jennifer on My Mind (1971)	Noel Black	Michael Brandon, Tippy Walker
42. Klute (1971)	Alan J. Pakula	Jane Fonda, Donald Sutherland
43. They Might Be Giants (1972)	Anthony Harvey	George C. Scott, Joanne Woodward
44. The Dealing (1972)	Paul Williams	Robert Lyons, John Lithgow, Barbara Hershey

Pictured above, Louis Goldman with, from left to right: Gregory Peck; Rex Harrison; Jane Fonda; his telephoto camera; Edward Steichen; John Frankenheimer

45. Fellini—Roma (1972)	Federico Fellini	Peter Gonzales
46. The Last American Hero (1973)	Lamont Johnson	Jeff Bridges, Valerie Perrine, Geraldine Fitzgerald
47. Jaws (1975)	Steven Spielberg	Robert Shaw, Roy Scheider, Richard Dreyfuss
48. All the President's Men (1976)	Alan J. Pakula	Robert Redford, Dustin Hoffman, Jason Robards, Jr.
49. Thieves (1977)	John Berry	Marlo Thomas, Charles Grodin
50. Billy Jack Goes to Washington (Not released)	Tom Laughlin	Tom Laughlin, Delores Taylor
51. The Turning Point (1977)	Herbert Ross	Shirley MacLaine, Anne Bancroft, Mikhail Baryshnikov, Leslie Browne
52. An Unmarried Woman (1977)	Paul Mazursky	Jill Clayburgh, Alan Bates, Michael Murphy
53. Matilda (1978)	Daniel Mann	Elliott Gould, Robert Mitchum
54. The Dain Curse (1978)	E. W. Swackhamer	James Coburn
55. Sooner or Later (1979)	Bruce Hart	Denise Miller, Rex Smith
56. The Rose (1979)	Mark Rydell	Bette Midler, Alan Bates
57. The Wanderers (1979)	Philip Kaufman	Ken Wahl, John Friedrich, Tony Kalem, Karen Allen
58. Just Tell Me What You Want (1980)	Sidney Lumet	Ali MacGraw, Alan King, Myrna Loy, Dina Merrill, Peter Weller, Keenan Wynn
59. Willie and Phil (1980)	Paul Mazursky	Margot Kidder, Michael Ontkean, Ray Sharkey
60. One-Trick Pony (1980)	Robert M. Young	Paul Simon, Blair Brown, Rip Torn
61. Prince of the City (1981)	Sidney Lumet	Treat Williams, Jerry Orbach
62. Blow Out (1981)	Brian De Palma	John Travolta, Nancy Allen
63. Deathtrap (1982)	Sidney Lumet	Michael Caine, Christopher Reeve, Dyan Cannon, Irene Worth
64. The Verdict (1982)	Sidney Lumet	Paul Newman, Charlotte Rampling, James Mason
65. Moscow on the Hudson (1984)	Paul Mazursky	Robin Williams, Maria Conchita Alonso
66. The Pope of Greenwich Village (1984)	Stuart Rosenberg	Mickey Rourke, Eric Roberts, Daryl Hannah
67. The Last Dragon (1985)	Michael Schultz	Taimak, Vanity, Julius J. Carry III
68. The Year of the Dragon (1985)	Michael Cimino	Mickey Rourke, Ariane

ACKNOWLEDGMENTS

Had Bob Morton known, when I submitted the idea for this book to him, how many other publishers I had already seen, perhaps he too might have turned it down with, "Interesting, but not for us." Instead, he said: "Let me think about it."

Ah...! For that alone, but also for his continuous, unfailing guidance and enthusiasm, my sincere gratitude.

Given the low priority of still photography on a movie, the job is an obstacle course even at the best of times. I am happy therefore to recognize those who have made it a little easier: It's of tremendous help when a director shows understanding; when an actor graciously gives me a few minutes of his time; when the focus-puller, eyes glued to the rolling camera, moves his elbow an inch so that I can shoot past it; or when a grip, sensing that I'm in trouble, sneaks up with a flag to shield my lens from a light kick.

For all these kindnesses and more, to all of you too numerous to single out, Thank You, Thank You.

FILM COPYRIGHTS